Praise for *America's Forgotten Student Population*

"*America's Forgotten Student Population* shines a spotlight on the many difficult challenges that GED recipients face when they pursue post-secondary education. But fortunately for the thousands of GED recipients in the U.S., this book highlights steps that colleges, schools, and communities can take to provide GED recipients with the kinds of information, support, and advice that can propel them to success in higher education and careers. This book makes clear that we should no longer consider GED recipients second to high school graduates; rather, with the right kinds of assistance and support they can be just as successful."
—**Betsy Brand**, *Executive Director, American Youth Policy Forum*

"*America's Forgotten Student Population* is an important addition to the analysis of the inadequate education of the American populace. It is critical that we understand and resolve the obstacles that lead to a high percentage of students dropping out rather than becoming significant contributors to our society."
—**Benjamin S. Carson Sr.**, *MD, Emeritus Professor of Neurosurgery, Oncology, Surgery, and Pediatrics at John Hopkins; Chairman and CEO, American Business Collaborative, LLC; Biography* Gifted Hands: The Ben Carson Story *by Sony Pictures*

"This book sheds some much-needed light on an understudied part of our higher education system. Researchers and policymakers should take heed of the potential to tap into the underutilized human capital present in GED completers as a means to improve national competitiveness and promote individual opportunity."
—**Nicole M. Chestang**, *PhD, Executive Vice President, GED Testing Service*

"Dr. Angela Long has a distinguished record of working with students from diverse populations. *America's Forgotten Student Population* provides critical strategies for those who recognize the importance and significance of post-secondary education for underserved students in our global society."
—**Kevin A. Christian**, *Senior Program Associate; Diversity, Inclusion, and Equity; American Association of Community Colleges*

"This important book provides a rich set of perspectives on the needs, aspirations, and, yes, potential for success of an often neglected population of college students: those who earned a GED instead of a high school diploma. It is a must-read for college educators who want to understand who these students are and how better to serve them."
—**Davis Jenkins**, *PhD, Senior Research Associate, Community College Research Center, Teachers College, Columbia University*

"*America's Forgotten Student Population: Creating a Path to College Success for GED®
Completers* is a remarkable book that combines groundbreaking research on the

lifelong learning of dropouts with very moving personal stories of students who have gone on to succeed in their lives. I strongly recommend this book to anyone wanting to understand the social, educational, and economic dimensions of these issues facing millions of adults in our country as well as what we can do about it."

—***Stephen Reder***, *PhD, Literacy, Language, and Technology Research Group, PSU;*
author, Literacy in America*; Professor of Linguistics, PSU*

"I'm pleased to see the release of Dr. Long's important book on *America's Forgotten Student Population*, as broadening educational opportunities have become an important component to our future. The research and observations presented within regarding these opportunities - and the role mentoring plays - can only benefit generations to come."

—***Dr. Nathan Whitaker***, *coauthor of the New York Times bestsellers*
The Mentor Leader, Quiet Strength, *and* Through My Eyes

AMERICA'S FORGOTTEN STUDENT POPULATION

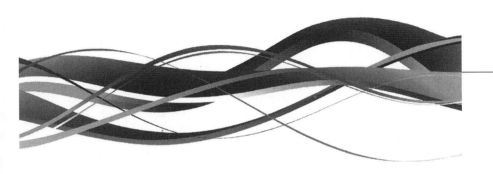

AMERICA'S FORGOTTEN STUDENT POPULATION

Creating a Path to College Success for GED® Completers

EDITED BY

Angela Long and
Christopher M. Mullin

Foreword by Story Musgrave,
Former U.S. Astronaut

STERLING, VIRGINIA

Published by Stylus Publishing, LLC.
22883 Quicksilver Drive
Sterling, Virginia 20166-2102

Library of Congress Cataloging-in-Publication Data
America's forgotten student population : creating a path to
college success for GED completers / Edited By Angela Long and
Christopher M. Mullin.
    p. cm.
Includes bibliographical references and index.
ISBN 978-1-62036-139-9 (cloth : alk. paper)
ISBN 978-1-62036-140-5 (pbk. : alk. paper)
ISBN 978-1-62036-141-2 (library networkable e-edition)
ISBN 978-1-62036-142-9 (consumer e-edition)
1. College dropouts—United States—Prevention. 2. College
students—United States. 3. Academic achievement—United States.
4. GED tests. I. Long, Angela. II. Mullin, Christopher M.
LC148.15.A54 2014
378.1'6913—dc23
                                                    2013040903

13-digit ISBN: 978-1-62036-139-9 (cloth)
13-digit ISBN: 978-1-62036-140-5 (paperback)
13-digit ISBN: 978-1-62036-141-2 (library networkable e-edition)
13-digit ISBN: 978-1-62036-142-9 (consumer e-edition)

Printed in the United States of America

All first editions printed on acid-free paper
that meets the American National Standards Institute
Z39-48 Standard.

First Edition, 2014

10 9 8 7 6 5 4 3 2 1

This book is dedicated to the more than 20 million Americans who have successfully earned a General Education Development (GED®) certificate in our country and are seeking to better their lives.
We congratulate you on your efforts and encourage you to never give up, because you have the potential in you to reach the greatest heights. And to those who work selflessly day by day in the education system to help these very same individuals achieve their life and career goals, thank you for your steadfast contributions.

Note: A portion of the proceeds from this book will be placed in a scholarship fund to assist students with GEDs enrolled in postsecondary education who have demonstrated leadership and scholarly achievement in higher education.

CONTENTS

EDITOR'S NOTE ON THE FOREWORD

American patriotism reached its zenith within each of the 48 states during World War II. Many young men between the ages of 16 and 17 falsified their birth years so that they could enlist in the five branches of the U.S. military: the army, the navy, the marine corps, the coast guard, and the army air corps. They dropped out of their respective high schools, went to "boot camps," and thereafter were transported to the European and Pacific war theaters to put their lives on the front lines to preserve America's freedom. But when those men returned, most of them no longer were in their early twenties. To enable those young warriors to compete for open positions in the marketplace, the U.S. Department of Veterans Affairs engaged the American Council on Education (ACE) to develop an education credential, comprising five proficiency tests that would be academically comparable to the traditional high school diploma.

The first group of veterans who took the ACE's battery of tests and earned a General Education Development (GED®) equivalency certificate did so in the year 1947. Following the Korean Conflict (1950–53), another group of veterans obtained GED certificates in lieu of high school diplomas. But today, the approximately 750,000 people who annually complete one or more of the five GED Content Tests (measuring skills in reading, writing, social studies, science, and math) are civilians who dropped out of high school for various reasons.

Few World War II veterans are alive today. And before long, there will be just a few veterans remaining who fought in the Korean Conflict. The foreword to this book is written by a military veteran of that era. During the first few months of Dr. Story Musgrave's senior year in high school, three of the bloodiest battles of the Korean Conflict were being fought—the Battle of Triangle Hill, the Battle of the Hook, and the Battle of Pork Chop Hill. In the spring of 1953 he dropped out of high school and enlisted in the U.S. Marine Corps prior to having earned a high school diploma. A few months later, he was sent to Korea to serve as an aircraft electrician and engine mechanic. He is a voice of someone who earned his GED certificate within six years after the inception of the first GED program.

As you will read in the foreword, Dr. Musgrave is a highly accomplished man. After obtaining his GED certificate, he went on to earn master's

degrees in mathematics, computer science, chemistry, physiology, and literature, as well as a doctorate in medicine from Columbia University College
of Physicians and Surgeons. In addition, he is the recipient of 20 honorary
doctorates. Dr. Musgrave was a NASA astronaut for more than 30 years,
served part-time as a trauma surgeon, and flew on six spaceflights. He performed the first shuttle spacewalk on *Challenger's* first flight, was a pilot
on an astronomy mission, conducted two classified Department of Defense
missions, was the lead spacewalker on the Hubble Telescope repair mission, and operated an electronic chip manufacturing satellite on *Columbia.*
Furthermore, he participated in the design and development of the Skylab
Program, the design and development of spacesuits and life support systems, and served as a spacecraft communicator aboard three space orbiters—
Challenger, *Atlantis*, and *Endeavor.* In 2003, Dr. Musgrave was honored to
be included in the NASA Hall of Fame. The "sky" certainly was not a limiting factor for Dr. Musgrave, nor should it be for any other GED certificate
holder both past and rising.

FOREWORD

I do not have a high school diploma; I have a GED® certificate, seven college degrees including a doctorate, and 20 honorary doctorates. In school I was an "at-huge-risk" kid. At risk because of family abuse, alcoholism, drug addiction, a broken home, and eventually leading to multiple suicides. At risk also because I was a very unusual kid and eccentrically brilliant. If I had had any mentor along the way who would have taken me in, understood me, understood my environment and my reactions to it, I would have been saved. But all the way through childhood and school I had no mentor, so I fell out along the roadside, as they now say, left behind.

This falling out of the mainstream happens to millions upon millions of folks who have great college, career, and social potential. It is just life—it happens. The causes are many: poverty, pregnancy, lack of support, continual moves, broken families, drug addiction, alcoholism, abuse, too much work, eccentric personal attributes, and so forth. These individuals have huge potential but they are branded with failure and a sense of hopelessness; without mentoring and intervention, this could be life's dead end for someone with the potential to make a great difference in the world.

I saw the way out. High school diploma or not, the U.S. Marines would educate me, put me to work, and give me critical responsibilities. I advanced rapidly and became a plane captain, the one who does the maintenance and coordinates all maintenance on an aircraft and signs off on all the certifications necessary for flight. I was responsible for the airworthiness of military aircraft at age 18. The military has played an important role in the history of the GED by helping folks who had volunteered to go to war prior to finishing high school get into college. The marine corps counseled me on the GED and administered the test to me. Now, as they say, GED in hand, the rest is history and what an adventure it has been.

Earning my GED instilled in me a sense of victory, in particular a sense of academic success, a sense of belonging to that community. I was proud of my efforts on the GED and proud of how I performed. Without a high school diploma I went confidently forward, got accepted to every college that I applied to, and again, as they say, the rest is history. All I needed was for that particular door of opportunity to open just one little bit and I would fly from there. Syracuse University gave me that opportunity, and the staff respected and loved me just like any other student; I made a varsity team my freshman year, made honors every semester, graduated with honors, and received an honorary doctorate later on.

There are millions of folks out there just like me who, through no fault of their own, have fallen out of the mainstream or have been forced out of it and who need that door of opportunity cracked just a little bit so that they too can follow their dreams (except, of course, spaceflight was not in my plans back then). In dramatic human terms that is what a GED is and that is how it works to open the doors of opportunity for millions.

Dr. Story Musgrave
Former U.S. Astronaut

The word *philanthropist* is used to describe a person who promotes human welfare and social reform. In the purest sense of this word, each person who contributed a chapter to this book is a philanthropist. Indeed, every one of the 12 contributors to this book sincerely believes he or she will be sufficiently rewarded if the conjoined sum of their cooperative endeavor is used as a foundational cornerstone upon which future paradigms, metrics, and models dealing with student persistence can be built. Simply put, their contributions were expressions of both their hearts and their minds. Surely every General Education Development (GED®) completer who enrolls in a community college during future years will become a beneficiary of the labors of the 12 philanthropists who made this book possible.

It is fair to say that *America's Forgotten Student Population: Creating a Path to College Success for GED® Completers* is unique in four respects. First, there is no other published book that deals exclusively with the topics of student attrition and persistence among GED completers who begin their postsecondary experience at a community college. Second, this book contains data, both quantitative and qualitative, heretofore unseen by virtually all community college presidents, as well as their deans of academic affairs— that is, the people who hold the power to alter their respective college's retention paradigms and attrition metrics. Third, this book not only yields fresh insights into the mind-set of college dropouts but also reveals the thinking of researchers and administrators who stand at the cutting edge of innovative program developments dealing with student persistence issues within two-year public institutions of higher learning. And, fourth, the 12 contributors add a multidimensional perspective on the dropout crisis now transpiring among GED completers during their first semester in college that otherwise could not be seen through a single writer's eyes. After all, who is better able to describe the inner joy a high school dropout experiences when handed a GED certificate than a high school dropout who earned that credential? In short, because "expression of differing perspectives" was one of the objectives of this book at its genesis, it is divided into four parts.

In Part One, "The Voice of the Researcher," the author of the first chapter is Christopher M. Mullin, my coeditor. Dr. Mullin has served as the program director for policy analysis at the American Association of Community Colleges for several years. Margaret Becker Patterson, the author of chapter 2, formerly served as the director of research at GED Testing, the only learner-centric organization that is nationally recognized in all 50 states, and currently holds the position of senior researcher at R-Ally™: Research Allies for Lifelong Learning, a private consulting firm that deals with adult learner policy issues. Wei Song, the author of chapter 3, currently serves as the director of data and analytics for the Achieving the Dream Foundation and formerly served as the director of research for the Council of Independent Colleges. All three of these contributors are nationally recognized for their expertise. It is noteworthy that Dr. Patterson spearheaded the seminal 2011 GED study entitled "Perceptions and Pathways," and that Dr. Song was a coauthor of that landmark study.

In Part Two, "The Voice of the Statewide Leader and Administrator," the perspectives of educators who hold important positions within the hierarchy of state leadership are set forth. The author of chapter 4, Helton "Hep" M. Aldridge, is nationally recognized for his innovative work in the development of a model teaching metric designed to promote student success at the community college level. He is also well known for working alongside other renowned experts, such as Dr. Terry O'Banion, former longtime president of the board of the League for Innovation in the Community College. In chapter 5, Mark A. Heinrich, chancellor of the Alabama Postsecondary Education System, focuses on the various developmental dilemmas commonly confronted by the majority of underprepared and at-risk students who enroll in community colleges. The author of chapter 6, Steve Dobo, is the chief executive officer of Zero Dropouts. He also founded the highly acclaimed dropout prevention program called Colorado Youth for a Change. In chapter 7, the perspective of the day-to-day workings of an innovative, as well as nationally recognized, adult transition program is seen through the eyes of Pamela Blumenthal, who currently serves as the director of Prep Alternative Programs at Portland Community College. The author of chapter 8 is Jackson Sasser, president of Santa Fe College in Gainesville, Florida, who was responsible for the implementation of a first-of-its-kind retention program for GED completers based on an innovative mentor paradigm that engages student leadership and faculty alike at the postsecondary level.

Part Three, "The Voice of the Student: Promoting Retention From a Student Leadership Perspective," contains the voices and perspectives of three people who either had earned a GED credential or had been involved in the development of methodologies aimed at reducing the unacceptably high attrition rates of GED enrollees. Chapter 9, written by GED certificate holder Leah Rapoza, tells the riveting story of her educational journey through college as support from college personnel served to overcome pressures from her family to drop out of school. Because of that support, she earned a master's degree in education and soon will be awarded a second master's degree in special education. Chapter 10 yields the perspective of a first-generation minority college student whose mother dropped out of high school due to an unplanned pregnancy but later earned a GED credential while rearing four children. Because of that experience and his admiration for his mother, Frederick Parks Jr., an excelling student who soon will be attending medical school, volunteered an untold number of hours while an undergraduate to help GED students persist in college. He was one of the student leaders who cofounded the Pathways to Persistence Scholars Program, which gained the attention of the U.S. Department of Education and other community colleges located in the southeastern part of the United States. And in chapter 11, Catlin Cade, peer connector coordinator and student leader, highlights the role of student leadership in partnering with offices such as Phi Theta Kappa to offer peer support and tutoring services for GED students so as to provide assistance toward successful degree attainment.

Besides writing the introduction to this book, I conducted an analysis of the differing voices, ferreting out any consensus opinions as to what each contributing writer jointly felt are feasible methodologies for enhancing the persistence and attainment rates of GED certificate holders who enroll in community colleges. In Part Four, "Conclusions and Recommendations," I provide a summary of my findings including the Five Factors for Improving Nontraditional Student Retention.

The reason that Portland Community College in Oregon, Aurora Community College in Colorado, Shelton State College in Alabama, and Santa Fe College in Florida are highlighted in this book is straightforward and simple: Each of these four public institutions developed innovative and successful paradigms for significantly reducing the number of dropouts among their GED demographic—programs that are beginning to catch the attention of other colleges throughout the United States. As you read each chapter, commonalities as to the retention methodologies employed by these four colleges will become increasingly evident.

Over the past two decades, critics of public education have loudly claimed that it is failing. Politicians blame school administrators for their inability to meet state and federal mandates, whereas school administrators say the primary causative force undergirding education's decline is diminished governmental funding. Moreover, politically conservative parents point to progressively minded teacher unions as the root cause of most of education's dropout problems. Finally, students say the dropout rate is currently at an epidemic level primarily because the curricula they are now being taught is boring and irrelevant.

Irrespective of which of these differing opinions comes closest to the truth, it is nearly impossible for policymakers to make good and well-reasoned decisions to reverse our nation's dropout crisis if there are no meaningful data upon which they can base their decisions. *America's Forgotten Student Population: Creating a Path to College Success for GED® Completers* unquestionably provides our nation's educational leadership with valuable and fundamental information that it has sorely needed in order to make those good decisions.

Angela Long

Dr. Angela Long
Chief Editor

Reference

GED Testing Service. (2011). *Perceptions and pathways: Life decisions of GED® test credential recipients from secondary to postsecondary education: A preliminary report.* Washington, DC: American Council on Education. Retrieved from http://www.gedtestingservice.com/uploads/files/e7ec4943a8688449a9d67ee9f1fda546.pdf

INTRODUCTION

Angela Long

Embarrassment, disappointment, and desolation can be felt by a student who has failed to meet the academic requirements of his or her institution. Imagine experiencing all of these emotions and not knowing how to get back on track.

—Christie Cruise, University of Illinois at Urbana-Champaign

There is truth in the adage that "change comes by crisis." History has shown that crises of all kinds often serve as the causative force that prompts government officials to enact changes in their governing rules. Indeed, if a particular crisis elicits a high degree of public outrage or fear, such as the 2001 destruction of the World Trade Center in New York or the 2012 school shooting at Sandy Hook Elementary School in Connecticut, legislators at all levels of government rush to pass more restrictive laws with the intent of swiftly assuaging the concerns of their respective electorates. Yet once in a while a crisis will occur that draws little attention from either legislators or the news media. The high attrition rates within community colleges provide an apt example of such a kind of crisis.

Between the years of 1947, when the first General Education Development (GED®) certificate was awarded, and the still-future year 2025, approximately 24 million residents of the United States will have earned a GED certificate. As a means of illustrating the magnitude of that number, it slightly exceeds the combined populations of the states of Maine, New Hampshire, Montana, South Dakota, Rhode Island, Wyoming, Idaho, Vermont, New Mexico, Kansas, West Virginia, Nebraska, Arkansas, Alaska, North Dakota, and Hawai'i (U.S. Census Quick Facts, 2012). Equally astonishing, out of those millions of men and women projected to earn their GED certificates during the next 10 years, roughly half will launch their postsecondary education in a community college. Thus, if we suppose that history repeats itself, we can reasonably predict that between 20% and 40% of those newly enrolled GED certificate holders will end their college experience within a time span of six months after having been matriculated, depending on the efficacy of the retention metrics of the college they attend.

But even if twice that number of GED students chose to drop out of college within half that period of time—roughly 500,000 men and women—that phenomenon still is likely to go unnoticed by an overwhelming majority of college personnel. Why? The answer is complex, but here is a partial explanation: The majority of college personnel tend to stereotype GED certificate holders as being academically underprepared for the rigors of postsecondary education.

Synonyms for *stigma* include *blemished, branded, dishonored, impure, shamed,* and *smirched.* Certainly all of these words tend to conjure up pejorative mental imagery. Some might argue that the phrase "GED dropout" elicits a similar stigmatizing impression. Indeed, the vast majority of those tens of millions of Americans who earned a GED certificate between 1950 and the present feel that college personnel unconsciously brand them as academically inferior to traditional high school graduates—as "quitters" who were not capable of effectively competing with other high school classmates who went on to earn a high school diploma. (If that statement strikes you as outrageous, ask a GED certificate holder if he or she likes being categorized as a "GED recipient.") Yet national data collected by the National Center for Education Statistics (NCES) reveals that GED certificate holders who persist to their second year of community college studies have accumulated grade point averages equal to those of their high school counterparts (Long, 2004).

What prompted educators at the college level to view GED certificate holders as being at far greater risk of dropping out of college than their high school counterparts? The U.S. Department of Education traditionally has categorized "nontraditional college students" as persons who possess one or more of these seven "factors" of predictive risk: (1) having delayed enrollment, (2) having children at home, (3) being a single parent, (4) attending college part-time, (5) being financially independent, (6) working full-time while enrolled in a postsecondary institution, and (7) being a GED certificate holder (NCES Fast Facts, 2002). Six of these criteria are reflective of specific *environmental traits,* that is, social and financial background characteristics commonly associated with these college-level at-risk students. But notice that GED certificate holders—persons classified as "at-risk" students due to their *academic accomplishment*—were included in this list. Since the GED certificate is designed to function as an *academic equivalent* of a high school diploma, why are GED certificate holders at greater risk of dropping out of community colleges than high school graduates when the law expressly requires GED students to demonstrate the same level of educational attainment as high school graduates in order for them to obtain a GED certificate?

(Perhaps the time has come to replace the traditional "GED" title with another abbreviation that is nonstigmatizing.)

Numerous studies over the past five decades have consistently produced the similar finding that Americans spend more money per capita on educating their adolescent and teenage children than any other nation in the world. However, current research shows that a majority of first-time college students take at least one remedial course. The common belief is that "underpreparedness" is a key causative force behind the high numbers of college dropouts, particularly at community colleges. With that thought in mind, pause for a moment to evaluate the import of these words from a research study conducted by the National Bureau of Economic Research, entitled "Development, Discouragement, or Diversion? New Evidence on the Effects of College Remediation": "Half of all college students take at least one remedial course as part of their postsecondary experience, despite mixed evidence on the effectiveness of this intervention. . . . We find that remediation does little to develop students' skills" (Scott-Clayton & Rodriguez, 2012).

As discussed in chapter 5, the traditional protocol that promotes the idea that remedial coursework is key to reducing the dropout rates among at-risk community college students may have, in reality, unwittingly served to produce the opposite effect (i.e., to increase dropout rates).

Over the past three decades, both the federal and state departments of education have sought to understand the causes of the escalating rates of high school attrition. Numerous theories have been advanced as possible explanations for this growing phenomenon among high school students. But oddly, community colleges have lagged behind in this effort to understand the "dropout crisis." If that statement seems unwarranted, consider the following words from an article in *U.S. News & World Report* entitled "Study: Community College Dropouts Prove Costly": "More than 40 percent of community colleges responding to a 2010 ACT survey have no one responsible for coordinating retention efforts; more than half have no goals for first-year student retention" (Jacobs, 2011).

The author of that news article cited data she retrieved from research conducted by several national organizations, including the American Association of Community Colleges (AACC), the American Institutes of Research (AIR), the U.S. Department of Education's NCES, Lumina Foundation's Achieving the Dream project, and Complete College America. The opening paragraph of this article is particularly attention-grabbing:

Fewer than 45 percent of college-ready students and just 20 percent of remedial students earn a certificate or degree in four years at Valencia College in Orlando, Fla. That's "nearly three times the rate" of similar urban community colleges and impressive enough to earn Valencia the first Aspen Prize for Community College Excellence, awarded Dec. 12 [2011] in Washington, D.C. (Jacobs, 2011)

It is the *reverse* of the numbers previously cited—that is, 55% and 80%—that ought to raise one's eyebrows. Indeed, if Valencia College were singled out as the best of America's 1,157 two-year public institutions of higher learning because it graduated nearly half of its student body with an associate's degree, then how are the 300 community colleges that fall within the bottom quartile of America's 1,157 community colleges doing with respect to their efficacy in reducing first-year student attrition? Regardless of how one chooses to answer that question, if the 2010 ACT survey is even marginally accurate—specifically, that 40% of community colleges have no one responsible for coordinating student retention efforts, and 50% of them have never developed a matrix to improve student retention—then it seems inarguable that America's educational system must undergo a metaphorical "rebirth" if it is to remain competitive in the global marketplace.

A *Terminus a Quo* Benchmark

A person who has "perspective" is said to be capable of viewing things in just proportion. In similar fashion, a person who possesses the ability to discern the true nature of something is said to have "perception." As such, the findings (i.e., "perceptions") of any given research project that involves observations of human behavior can be skewed away from reality if the researcher's "perspective" lacks sufficient breadth and scope. Of course, the most practical means for averting such research deficiencies is to conduct observations through several sets of trained eyes. Thus, the contributing writers who made this book possible—policy analysts, researchers, practitioners, college administrators, and student leaders—collectively produced *a terminus a quo* benchmark that can serve as a springboard for educators to develop more efficacious sets of metrics to enhance student persistence and attainment. (The word *benchmark* denotes the idea of something that serves as a standard point of reference for decision making, and the Latin phrase *terminus a quo* means "starting point.")

Without question, all of the educators, policy analysts, researchers, and administrators who participated in the development of *America's Forgotten Student Population: Creating a Path to College Success for GED® Completers* are people specially gifted with an abundance of "perspective" and "perception." In addition to holding positions of high authority in education, all of them also are nationally recognized by their peers as both experts and policy innovators in their respective fields of specialty—people who stand on the cutting edge of exploration and new understandings of the issues associated with student attrition, persistence, and attainment.

Global automotive manufacturers long ago discovered that some of the best ideas for achieving better productivity at lower costs originated from their assembly-line workers. In like manner, when educators and analysts seek to discover the differing thought patterns that swirl about in the collective mind-set of GED college dropouts, who is better qualified to speak about the self-doubt that GED students experience than GED students who themselves struggled with self-doubt? Chapter 9 of this book will take you on a fascinating journey into the mind-set of a GED student who battled the same obstacles that derail so many people belonging to this demographic group. Furthermore, you will hear the voices of engaged student leaders who experimented with different approaches for increasing the persistence rates of GED certificate holders who enroll in two-year public institutions of higher learning.

When you have finished reading the first three chapters of the book, you already will have garnered a plethora of research findings far more comprehensive than anything available on the Internet. And for those readers who are college administrators, before you turn the last page of chapter 6 you will already be thinking about creative ways to bolster the rates of persistence and attainment at your own college. Once you have finished reading the last chapter, you will want to pass this book on to your colleagues.

Many college personnel, including some college presidents, commonly believe that GED certificate holders are not academically competitive with high school graduates. Yet, remarkably, when asked how many of their GED population drop out either before or immediately after their first term or semester in college, only a small percentage of college administrators are able to point to verifiable data collected by their institutional research personnel that answer that question. Perhaps Mark Schneider (2011), vice president of American Institutes for Research, aptly summed up the core of this problem with this brief statement: "Data collection and data dissemination are still in the Dark Ages." His rather brusque comment raises this intriguing question: How is it possible for analysts and administrators to formulate an effective retention paradigm aimed at the "at-risk" GED college demographic if they do not know what percentage of their GED students are dropping out of college? The best answer to that question: It is not possible!

Today's best scholars tend to stand upon the shoulders of the preceding generation of scholars. Up until just recently, the number of shoulders upon which educators could stand while examining data concerning the causal forces that induce GED certificate holders to prematurely drop out of community colleges were, to be blunt, few indeed. But *America's Forgotten Student Population: Creating a Path to College Success for GED® Completers* significantly changes that condition. If the data collection and data dissemination concerning our nation's dropout crisis was still in "the Dark Ages" as recently as 2011 (as Mark Schneider asserted), then it is fair to say that this book is a giant leap toward "enlightenment." And in the same metaphorical vein, it also serves as a sturdy set of "shoulders" upon which future researchers and educators can squarely stand.

References

Jacobs, J. (2011, December 16). Study: Community college dropouts prove costly. *U.S. News & World Report.* Retrieved from http://www.usnews.com/education/best-colleges/articles/2011/12/16/study-community-college-dropouts-prove-costly

Long, A. (2004). *Community college attrition of GED certificate holders and regular high school graduates: A comparative study using national BPS data.* Ann Arbor, MI: UMI Dissertation Services.

National Center for Education Statistics Fast Facts. (2002). Washington, DC: National Center for Statistics, U.S. Department of Education (NCES 96-155). Retrieved from http://nces.ed.gov/fastfacts/

Schneider, M. (2011, October). The hidden costs of community colleges. *American Institutes for Research.* Retrieved from http://www.air.org/files/AIR_Hidden_Costs_of_Community_Colleges_Oct2011.pdf

Scott-Clayton, J., & Rodriguez, O. (2012, August). *Development, discouragement, or diversion? New evidence on the effects of college remediation* (NBER Working Paper No. 18328). Retrieved from http://www.nber.org/papers/w18328

U.S. Census Quick Facts. (2012). *State and county quick facts* [Data file]. Retrieved from http://quickfacts.census.gov/qfd/states/00000.html

PART ONE

THE VOICE OF THE RESEARCHER

I

IDLE ASSETS

An Examination of America's Underdeveloped Capital

Christopher M. Mullin

Show me a man who never makes a mistake, and I'll show you a man who never does anything.

—President Theodore Roosevelt

As the American economy revs up in response to the Great Recession, we need to be sure it has the workforce it needs. Throughout recent history there have always been more workers than jobs available; however, this trend has now shifted, with the supply of highly skilled workers lower than the number of jobs to be filled (Carnevale & Rose, 2011). This is especially true for the workers' business and industry needs—those with a postsecondary education. Carnevale, Smith, and Strohl (2010) estimate that 62% of workers need to have a postsecondary credential.

In light of this demand, institutions of higher education are reexamining their offerings to ensure that those students who enter obtain a credential. Aside from structural changes needed to meet the increased demand for more college credential holders, colleges are looking harder at the populations they serve to determine which groups have been less successful than others and what actions need to be taken to help them become successful.

This book is focused on one such historically underexamined population on college campuses: students with high school equivalencies such as General Education Development (GED®) diplomas. This chapter sets the foundation for such an examination by giving a general description of GED students.

It then examines the implications associated with the premature departure of these students from college campuses and concludes with considerations for the future.

Who Are GED Students?

Data reported by the GED Testing Service® provide the first necessary points of information about the GED population. Primary among them, as illustrated in Figure 1.1, are two descriptors of the average test taker: They are in their midtwenties and have achieved a 10th-grade level of education. Taken together, these two data points frame what can only be considered a decade of disaster, starting with the departure from high school at roughly age 16 to the reengagement with formal learning that signifies a minimal level of knowledge at the age of 25.[1] During this time many life choices are made that cause those who return to college to be different from their peers; primary among the differences is that nearly half have dependents as compared with only a quarter of students with a high school diploma.[2]

The item in Figure 1.1 that has exhibited the greatest change over time is the percentage of test takers who expressed intent to engage in further study,

Figure 1.1 Data on GED test takers: 1958 to 2011.

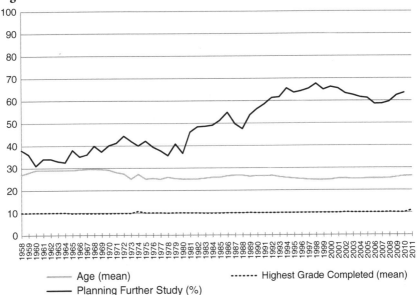

Source. GED Testing Service (2011, 2012).

rising from 38% in 1958 to 64% in 2010. Starting in 2002, the GED Testing Service disaggregated the data in terms of why GED test takers who passed the test took the test, consistently finding that the first reason was to obtain personal satisfaction (~50%), the second was to get a better job (~40%), and the third was to attend a community college (~30%). It is indeed the case that many GED students do enroll in college; in the 2007–08 academic year, 6% of all students in higher education had earned a GED and 8.2% of community college students had a GED.[3]

Despite the desire to earn a college credential, GED college students, on average, stumble right out of the gate: Within two years of starting at a community college, 56.7% of GED students were no longer enrolled.[4] Furthermore, while data indicate that they can be successful in college, less than half of students entering college with a GED completed a college credential within six years of starting (see Table 1.1).

Assuming the behaviors for this cohort were consistent, 1.16 million GED students who started at a community college and an additional 754,609 GED students attending other colleges over the past decade will not earn a college credential within six years of first enrolling (see Figure 1.2). In total, just over 2 million GED students who started college in the past decade have not, or will not, take the next step along the continuum of educational attainment by earning a college credential.

The annual attrition of GED students is our problem. The impact of this failure cannot be understated.

GED College Dropouts

The attrition of 2 million GED students is not a small number. Perhaps more so than for other populations, the attrition of these students may be more directly related to institutional actions given the fact that these students have exhibited personal responsibility and resilience in returning to education after having not completed high school on the common path. As such, it is more palatable to consider the attrition of these students to be an institutional, personal, and societal loss.

Estimating the loss associated with student attrition is difficult but not impossible. Given that community colleges serve the greatest number of GED students, and the resulting data are more robust, I estimate the costs associated with the early departure of 1.16 million GED students from community colleges at $1.359 billion in tuition and fees and state appropriations.[5] That is a staggering cost.[6]

While these costs are felt by the sponsoring entities (i.e., taxpayers and students, many of whom are also taxpayers), there is another way to look

TABLE 1.1

Six-Year Cumulative Persistence and Attainment Student Outcomes, by Initial College Attended for GED Students Starting College in 2003–04

| | *Cumulative Persistence and Attainment Anywhere 2008–09* | | | | | |
| | *Earned a College Credential* | | | *Yet to Earn a College Credential* | | |
Initial College Attended	Attained Bachelor's Degree (%)	Attained Associate's Degree (%)	Attained Certificate (%)	No Degree, Still Enrolled (%)	No Degree, Left Without Return (%)	Total (%)
Total (all colleges)	2.7	10.6	20.7	16.5	49.5	100
Community colleges	—	11.2	11.7	19.3	56.7	100
All other colleges	—	9.9	30.8	13.3	41.6	100

Note. Em dash denotes unstable estimate.
Source. Author's analysis of Beginning Postsecondary Student Longitudinal Study 04:09 (NCES, 2013b).

Figure 1.2 Estimate of the number of GED students who will not complete a college credential within six years of starting, by year of initial enrollment and college type (includes students still enrolled).

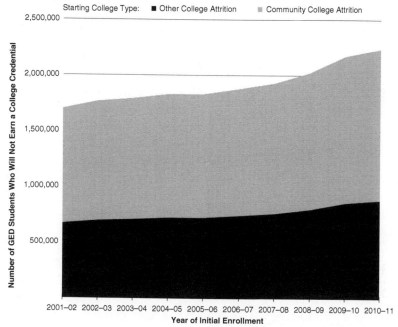

Source. Snyder, Dillow, & Hoffman (2007); Snyder & Dillow (2012); author's analysis of Beginning Postsecondary Student Longitudinal Study 04:09 (NCES, 2013b).

at these data: the amount of college revenue associated with getting these students to earn an associate's degree. An estimate of institutional revenues associated with getting the 1.16 million GED students at community colleges to earn an associate's degree is $578 million in constant 2011 dollars.

The collective impact of the nearly 2 million GED students not earning an associate's degree in the year 2011 alone was $4.9 billion in earnings.[7] Consequently, roughly $361.5 billion in earnings (2011 dollars) are to be unrealized.[8]

Aside from private returns to education, there are public fiscal returns as well (Baum, Ma, & Payea, 2010; McMahon, 2009). Mullin and Phillippe (2013) estimated the differences in taxes paid for each level of educational attainment in 2011. When their values are applied to the lost earnings for this group of students, the result is a loss of $3.6 billion in taxes paid for 2011 alone and $28.7 billion lost over 30 years (in 2011 dollars).[9]

Looking Ahead

Increasingly public policy decisions, such as the removal of the ability to benefit from provisions that provide a pathway to federal student aid for students without a high school diploma or its equivalent, are framing college education as a reward rather than an opportunity. This refined focus on high school equivalency as the requisite starting point for college opportunities is solidifying the role of the credential-based progression of educational attainment as an on-ramp to college. However, there are large numbers of Americans who have aged out of the traditional on-ramp to college (high school).

The sheer number of people without a high school credential over the age of 18 was a staggering 30.9 million in 2011; two-thirds, or about 20 million, have completed some high school, with another 10.8 million having elementary education as their highest level of attainment (see Table 1.2). There does not seem to be a substantial difference between genders, but nearly one third of all Hispanics (34.5%) have less than a high school education as compared to less than 1 in 10 White students (8.5%). These data are especially troubling because projections indicate that current populations with low high school attainment rates will become an increasingly larger percentage of the American population in the coming decades (Prescott & Bransberger, 2012).

There are nascent efforts by other entities to offer high school equivalency exams in addition to the GED. These new exams, the High School Equivalency Test (HiSET®), developed by the Educational Testing Service (ETS), and the Test Assessing Secondary Completion (TASC™), developed by CTB/McGraw-Hill, have the ability to provide even more opportunity for the large number of students who seek to reengage with learning and prepare for the education and training that community colleges and other colleges provide.

America has a substantial amount of underdeveloped capital. The GED student body provides one avenue to develop this capital, and, as will be discussed, there are ways to ensure that a high school equivalency is not the last step on a student's progression of educational attainment. By activating our nation's idle assets, the country will benefit from increased economic security and reinforce an important construct of American society: mobility.

Notes

1. Economists term the period before the age of 25 as *turbulence* (Kerckhoff, 2002).

2. Author's analysis of Beginning Postsecondary Student Longitudinal Study 04:09 data (NCES, 2013b).

TABLE 1.2

Highest Level of Educational Attainment for Persons Ages 18 and Over, by Gender and Race/Ethnicity in 2011

Demographics	*Highest Level of Educational Attainment*						Total
	Some Elementary		*Some High School*		*Subtotal*		
Total	10,849,000	(4.7%)	20,003,000	(8.7%)	30,852,000	(13.3%)	231,194,000
Gender							
Male	5,464,000	(4.9%)	10,302,000	(9.2%)	15,766,000	(14.0%)	112,301,000
Female	5,385,000	(4.5%)	9,701,000	(8.2%)	15,086,000	(12.7%)	118,893,000
Race/Ethnicity							
White	3,373,000	(2.2%)	9,987,000	(6.4%)	13,360,000	(8.5%)	156,709,000
Black	885,000	(3.3%)	3,517,000	(13.2%)	4,402,000	(16.5%)	26,684,000
Hispanic	5,815,000	(17.9%)	5,361,000	(16.5%)	11,176,000	(34.5%)	32,434,000
Asian	668,000	(6.2%)	600,000	(5.5%)	1,268,000	(11.7%)	10,819,000

Source. Author's analysis of Current Population Survey Data as presented in Snyder and Dillow (2012).

3. Author's analysis of National Postsecondary Student Aid Study 04/08 data (NCES, 2013b).

4. Author's analysis of Beginning Postsecondary Student Longitudinal Study 04:09 data (NCES, 2013b).

5. Data are in 2011 constant dollars. This estimate was determined by taking various analyses dependent on data for tuition and fee sticker prices as published in annual publications of the College Board's Trends in Student Pricing, public subsidy costs derived from data presented in the Integrated Postsecondary Education Data System (NCES, 2013a), earned credit distributions for GED populations at community colleges in 2003–04 from the Beginning Postsecondary Student Longitudinal Study 04:09 (NCES, 2013b), and adjustments from the U.S. Department of Labor's Consumer Price Index calculator (www.bls.gov/cpi). The assumption was made that the resulting cost per GED student head count in 2003–04 was consistent across the other nine cohorts. This estimate is in the middle of the range of earned credits for those who did not earn a credential in six years. One may arrive at a higher or lower estimate depending on whether they believe students within credit bands took the maximum or minimum level of credits.

6. Technically there is an economic return for students as they move from being high school completers to students with "some college." Yet, the "some college" category is a black box we have yet to decipher. At present there is work under way through the Interagency Working Group on Expanded Measures of Enrollment and Attainment (http://nces.ed.gov/surveys/gemena). It is for this reason that this chapter focuses on getting students to complete an associate's degree.

7. This value is the difference in estimated total annual earnings for this group of associate's degree holders of $76,496,769,024 and those with some college, at $71,616,115,792.

8. This value is the result of the difference in lifetime earnings between associate's degree holders and those with some college in 2009 as estimated by Carnevale, Rose, and Cheah (2011) after adjusting for inflation using the Consumer Price Index. That difference was then multiplied by the total number of GED students leaving college (1,915,384).

9. The estimate of lost lifetime earnings was multiplied by the estimated percentage increase in taxes by moving from "some college" to an associate's degree holder, which was 7.9%.

References

Baum, S., Ma, J., & Payea, K. (2010). *Education pays 2010: The benefits of higher education for individuals and society* (Trends in Higher Education Series). Washington, DC: College Board.

Carnevale, A. P., & Rose, S. J. (2011). *The undereducated American*. Washington, DC: Center on Education and the Workforce, Georgetown University.

Carnevale, A. P., Rose, S. J., & Cheah, B. (2011, August). *The college payoff: Education, occupations, lifetime earnings.* Washington, DC: Center on Education and the Workforce, Georgetown University.

Carnevale, A. P., Smith, N., & Strohl, J. (2010, June). *Help wanted: Projections of jobs and education requirements through 2018.* Washington, DC: Center on Education and the Workforce, Georgetown University.

GED Testing Service. (2011). *2010 GED testing program statistical report.* Washington, DC: American Council on Education.

GED Testing Service. (2012). *2011 GED testing program statistical report.* Washington, DC: American Council on Education.

Kerckhoff, A. C. (2002). The transition from school to work. In J. T. Mortimer & R. W. Larson (Eds.), *The changing adolescent experience: Societal trends and the transition to adulthood* (pp. 52–87). New York, NY: Cambridge University Press.

McMahon, W. L. (2009). *Higher learning, greater good: The private and social benefits of higher education.* Baltimore, MD: Johns Hopkins University Press.

Mullin, C. M., & Phillippe, K. (2013, February). *Community college contributions* (Policy Brief 2013-01PB). Washington, DC: American Association of Community Colleges.

National Center for Education Statistics (NCES). (2013a). *Integrated Postsecondary Education Data System* [Data files]. Available from http://www.nces.ed.gov/ipeds

National Center for Education Statistics (NCES). (2013b). *Powerstats* [Data file]. Available from http://nces.ed.gov/datalab/

Prescott, B. T., & Bransberger, P. (2012, December). *Knocking at the college door: Projections of high school graduates* (8th ed.). Boulder, CO: Western Interstate Commission for Higher Education.

Snyder, T. D., & Dillow, S. A. (2012, June). *Digest of education statistics: 2011* (NCES 2012-001). Washington, DC: U.S. Department of Education, Institute of Education Sciences, National Center for Education Statistics (NCES).

Snyder, T. D., Dillow, S. A., & Hoffman, C. M. (2007). *Digest of education statistics: 2006* (NCES 2007-017). Washington, DC: U.S. Department of Education, Institute of Education Sciences, National Center for Education Statistics (NCES).

AMERICA'S UNTAPPED RESOURCE

Taking a Closer Look at GED® Student Populations

Margaret Becker Patterson

You can teach a student a lesson for a day; but if you can teach him to learn by creating curiosity, he will continue the learning process as long as he lives.

—Clay P. Bedford

As of 2010, an estimated 39–40 million Americans had not completed high school in the United States and were at least 16 years of age (GED Testing Service®, 2012; Quigley, Patterson, & Zhang, 2011). Roughly one in six American adults are lacking a high school diploma and face limited prospects in life without additional education (Quigley et al., 2011). With further education, they comprise an untapped resource with vast potential.

One option to augment their prospects is taking the General Education Development (GED®) test before beginning college. The number of GED passers now exceeds 19 million adults (cumulatively since 1947; GED Testing Service, 2012). Because a growing population of adults with GED credentials aims toward college, in particular community college (Reder, 2007), learning about how they access and succeed in college is critical (Quigley et al., 2011). The purpose of this chapter is to provide an overview of adults entering college with GED credentials, to show how they differ from traditional and nontraditional college students with high school diplomas, and to define their needs and recommendations to community college staff and administrators.

What many community college staff and administrators may not realize is that adults come to GED testing for a host of reasons and through a variety of routes. Although numerous adults seek the credential to obtain employment, the most prevalent reason is to pursue further education. About two-thirds of GED passers give further education as a reason for GED testing (GED Testing Service, 2012), and a substantial percentage follow up on their college-going plans (Crissey & Bauman, 2012; Patterson, Zhang, Song, & Guison-Dowdy, 2010; Zhang, Guison-Dowdy, Patterson, & Song, 2011). Recently the U.S. Census Bureau reported that slightly more than 42% of adults ages 18 and above with GED or alternative credentials had attended "some college" (Crissey & Bauman, 2012).

While most GED passers leave high school early, typically in 11th grade (GED Testing Service, 2012), some complete 12th grade. The latter group comprises those who take the GED test as homeschoolers, youth with disabilities who want to show they have attained basic skills, or traditional 12th graders who do not meet administrative requirements to graduate. Others are immigrants with credentials from their home countries in need of an accepted U.S. credential (Patterson et al., 2010).

Crossing the Bridge Study

Further data on the actual population of GED test takers fill in the enrollment picture. According to GED Testing Service's *Crossing the Bridge* research, in a cohort of approximately half a million adults testing in 2003 and matched with postsecondary data from the National Student Clearinghouse, 43% of GED passers enrolled in postsecondary education by 2009. Roughly the same percentage (43%) of those passing in 2004 participated in college by 2010 (Patterson et al., 2010; Zhang et al., 2011). These figures are important because they point to the full number of adults who take a major high school equivalency test nationally (i.e., the population of potential future college students via a major alternative route), and because they estimate the extent to which the population of GED passers goes to college.

Crossing the Bridge reports that the characteristics of those entering college with GED credentials were consistent in the first and second years. The median age of enrollees in both cohorts was 20 years. About half of enrollees in postsecondary education were female, which represents a disproportionately high rate of female enrollment given that three-fifths of GED passers were male. An estimated three in five enrollees were White, and one in six was either African American or Hispanic, with the Hispanic enrollment proportion increasing from 14% to 17% from 2003 to 2004.

Enrollment Timing

The *Crossing the Bridge* study also reports how soon passers enroll in postsecondary education after GED testing, which is useful to those community college staff involved in recruitment efforts. Employing an analytical technique known as survival analysis, Patterson et al. (2010) found that most adults with GED credentials (about 72%) enrolled within three years of testing, with peak enrollment occurring at 14 months after testing. The second-year report offered similar findings, with 69% entering college within three years and peak enrollment occurring at 15 months (Zhang et al., 2011). Although GED passers may need some time to make the decision to go to college and to actually enroll, the data from both cohorts indicate that they tend not to delay entry very long.

Institutional Level

Another research area in the *Crossing the Bridge* study dealt with postsecondary institutional level. Do GED passers tend to enroll in postsecondary certificate or associate's degree programs in community colleges, or, like traditional high school graduates, do they more often pursue bachelor's degrees in four-year institutions (Aud, KewalRamani, & Frohlich, 2011)? This question has key implications for postsecondary institutions—especially community colleges—because approximately 1 out of every 12 entering first-year college students has GED credentials, according to estimates from the *Beginning Postsecondary Students Longitudinal Study* of 2003–04 (BPS; Zhang et al., 2011).

Both the first- and second-year *Crossing the Bridge* summaries reported that the vast majority of GED passers chose the former: Seventy-eight percent of the 2003 cohort and 77% of the 2004 cohort enrolled in postsecondary programs of up to two years in length (Patterson et al., 2010; Zhang et al., 2011). A follow-up study to the first-year report (Patterson, 2010) revealed that they entered predominantly public two-year colleges (i.e., community colleges). Figures from these reports indicate that an estimated 100,000 or more new GED passers per cohort year could be expected to flow into community colleges across the United States—not including hundreds of thousands of GED passers with postsecondary potential from previous decades.

Persistence to Graduation

Of huge concern in both *Crossing the Bridge* reports and later follow-up analyses is persistence to graduation. The graduation rate for GED-passer postsecondary enrollees in both cohorts was a staggeringly low 12% (Patterson et al., 2010; Zhang et al., 2011). About half of adults with GED credentials left college after the first semester, and 62% overall dropped out during the period of study. It is certainly reasonable for community college administrators to wonder what happened with student persistence, particularly given GED passers' substantial interest in college at the time of GED testing and the moderately high college entry rate.

Several demographic and academic characteristics provide information about persistence to graduation. In the 2003 cohort of GED passers, female, White, or older students who attended college programs of two years or less had higher odds of graduating from community college, as did students who completed 12th grade and those who enrolled full-time in college (Patterson, 2010). Data from the 2004 cohort suggest that persistence may also be related to increasing levels of educational experience (R-Ally™, 2012). A higher grade level completed while still in high school was also positively associated with total number of college semesters enrolled for GED passers in the 2004 cohort. This relationship implies that students completing 11th or 12th grade, who have more educational experience than their peers completing lower grades, may be ready to persist in college (R-Ally™, 2012).

GED passers may experience education gradually, sometimes even step-by-step, as they gain educational maturity. In addition to the 62% who dropped out and the 12% who graduated, 26% remained enrolled in college during the period of study in both cohorts; if all of these students joined the 12% of graduates at a later date, the potential proportion of graduates could be as high as 38% (Patterson et al., 2010; R-Ally™, 2012; Zhang et al., 2011). GED passers appear to need extended time, perhaps twice the traditionally expected time to earn a degree (Bound, Lovenheim, & Turner, 2010; Horn, 2010). How much time does it take? Patterson (2010) wrote about community college graduates with GED credentials:

> More than half of the [community college graduates] received associate degrees after an average of four years; another third earned certificates, on average within a year to year and a half after enrolling. These results highlight the role of extended time, with an average graduate tending to require nearly twice the time to graduate from a postsecondary program. Administrators and staff of college programs that are traditionally considered two-year programs need to be aware of these findings when planning or enhancing programs of study and recruiting adults with GED credentials. (p. 16)

Enrolling for at least 8 semesters may serve as a tipping point for persistence to graduation, according to 2004 cohort data (R-Ally™, 2012). Graduation rates were much higher for GED passers enrolling for 8–14 semesters (nearly half graduated) than for students enrolling all other semester lengths; less than 3% of GED passers who enrolled for a single semester graduated from their postsecondary program (R-Ally™, 2012). These data imply that persistence across multiple semesters is closely tied to college graduation.

Two last components of persistence to graduation are GED test-taker intent and timing of enrollment. In the 2004 cohort of the *Crossing the Bridge* study, GED passers who reported their two- or four-year college intent at higher rates when testing stayed in college more semesters than GED passers who did not test specifically to enter college but perhaps decided to enroll after testing timing of enrollment (R-Ally™, 2012). In addition, the largest number of GED passers—about 50,000 per semester—enrolled in college during the 2004–05 and 2005–06 academic years (referred to as early enrollees), while approximately 38,000 GED passers per semester enrolled in the final two academic years of the study, 2008–09 and 2009–10 (referred to as late enrollees). Demographically early enrollees were similar to late enrollees, yet their outcomes differed; of early enrollees 45% graduated from college, in contrast with 33% of late enrollees. One possible explanation for the difference is that early enrollees capitalized on the momentum of passing the GED test by enrolling right away and felt motivated to complete a postsecondary program. Another explanation for the difference could be that early enrollees had more time to graduate from their postsecondary programs than late enrollees, who perhaps continued after the period of the *Crossing the Bridge* study (R-Ally™, 2012).

Journeys Through College Studies

Community college staff and administrators regularly meet new students who have taken traditional and nontraditional routes to college: How do GED passers entering college compare with traditional high school graduates? Earlier in this chapter, entering first-year college students sampled in the federal BPS from 2004 were referenced (Zhang et al., 2011). Using BPS data from 1996 and 2001, Reder (2007) had first reported on the contrast of GED credential recipients and traditional high school graduates transitioning to postsecondary programs. The recent availability of 2004 BPS data, with later waves in 2006 and 2009, suggested an update of Reder's comparison. Thus, on the heels of the *Crossing the Bridge* study, the American Council on Education (ACE) published two follow-up reports, *Journeys Through College* and *Journeys Through College 2* (Guison-Dowdy & Patterson, 2011a, 2011b). The first report compared transitions and outcomes, and the second the postsecondary experiences of first-year college students by educational background.

Transitions and Outcomes

A key message from *Journeys Through College* is that adults with GED credentials and traditional high school graduates are surprisingly alike in many fundamental ways when compared demographically and by other background characteristics in their transitions to college. Similar to what was reported in the *Crossing the Bridge* study, BPS findings confirm that more females than males, more White students than African American or Hispanic students, and more primary English speakers than speakers of other languages enroll in college. In addition, both groups of adults tended to first enroll in colleges with programs of two years or less (though traditional high school graduates were much more likely to directly enter a four-year college or university than GED passers). Furthermore, in making a college selection, location and course offerings were of primary importance to both groups, at similar rates (Guison-Dowdy & Patterson, 2011a). The authors wrote,

> What is remarkable about these findings, with the exception of age . . . , is how similar beginning college students were. ***It is crucial for educators . . . to realize that their message about the potential benefits of a college education is reaching many ears.*** . . . More outreach to potential students from [diverse gender, cultural, and linguistic] subgroups is needed to encourage them to respond to the message about the benefits of postsecondary programs. (p. 30; emphasis in original)

Other similarities that first-year college students from either background shared were common goals for their postsecondary experiences. The most cited reason for entering college for both groups was to secure a steady job. A second frequently shared goal was being able to afford leisure time, followed by being acknowledged as an expert or having a family (Guison-Dowdy & Patterson, 2011b).

A first substantial difference between the two education backgrounds is age. Adults in the BPS study with GED credentials were 24 years old on average, compared with 18 years for traditional high school graduates. Moreover, unlike traditional graduates, adults with GED credentials tended to be financially independent, employed full-time, single parents, or at much greater risk for college dropout. Adults with GED credentials also had nearly twice the rate of disabilities (17%) as their peers who graduated from high school (10%). GED passers tended to attend institutions with lower tuition and fees than traditional high school graduates did. More than a third of GED passers and half of traditional high school graduates in the BPS survey completed their college programs (Guison-Dowdy & Patterson, 2011a). The authors stated several implications of the differences:

> One important distinction is that GED test passers tended to be older than traditional high school graduates. . . . Those who counsel adult learners in [an older] age group need to have a frank conversation with them about their postsecondary goals and how to reach them. ***Colleges that serve adult learners need to offer ample information, guidance, and programs geared toward the realities of GED test passers' lives.***
>
> One implication of the higher rate of disabilities for GED test passers than for traditional high school graduates is that many postsecondary students with disabilities may be newly diagnosed as adults and unaware of available services to students with disabilities. Even students who have received accommodations in public schools for many years may be unfamiliar with college services and with the differences in levels of support between K–12 schools and colleges. ***The higher rate of disabilities among GED test passers calls for appropriate, tailored services to accommodate these students' needs and ensure that they work toward a postsecondary credential under the most equitable conditions possible.*** (Guison-Dowdy & Patterson, 2011a, p. 30; emphasis in original)

Financial Aid

One need that college students from either background had in common was financial aid; approximately 85% of either group applied for financial aid to help them through college. On average, however, adults with GED credentials received approximately 25% less in financial aid than their counterparts with traditional high school diplomas. Guison-Dowdy and Patterson (2011b) wondered whether the difference might be attributed to GED passers' inability to navigate through financial aid requirements or to their selection of larger, public colleges, which would tend to be less expensive and thus require less investment. Another explanation might be GED passers' caution about taking on college debt (Guison-Dowdy & Patterson, 2011b). Regardless of the explanation, community college staff cannot assume that GED passers walking through their doors understand where and how to access financial aid.

Developmental Instruction

An unexpected finding of *Journeys Through College 2* was that approximately 21% of first-year college students—from either background—took developmental coursework. About 18% of students with GED credentials took developmental mathematics, compared with nearly 17% of students with traditional diplomas; the percentage for writing was 8% in both groups. "This finding represents a shift," explained Guison-Dowdy and Patterson (2011b,

p. 26), "as GED test passers traditionally demonstrated levels of skills requiring developmental coursework more often than those of traditional high school graduates." The similar percentages also call into question whether high school graduates and GED passers alike are fully prepared for credit-bearing courses in postsecondary programs. It is not yet known whether college students with GED credentials who participate in developmental education experience differences in persistence, graduation, and college debt.

Attendance and Stop-Out

Another similarity that first-year college students from either background experienced was in attendance intensity. The majority of GED passers (60%) and traditional high school graduates (70%) attended college full-time. From 2003 to 2009, 44% of GED passers and 51% of traditional high school graduates maintained full-time attendance (Guison-Dowdy & Patterson, 2011b). These high percentages are a positive sign for persistence, especially given the connection between full-time student status and graduation noted earlier in *Crossing the Bridge* reports.

Stop-out (defined in BPS as a break of five months or more in enrollment) is a valid concern because students who stop out of college are at risk of not completing postsecondary programs. In the first three years of college attendance, about 80% of students in the BPS study experienced no stop-out, regardless of educational background (Guison-Dowdy & Patterson, 2011b). This percentage is in strong contrast with that of *Crossing the Bridge*; in that study, 62% of students enrolling in postsecondary education left and did not return.

College Success and Employment

Guison-Dowdy and Patterson (2011b) noted the importance of cumulative grade point average (GPA) to college success. What college GPA levels should community college staff and administrators anticipate from GED passers? Another unexpected similarity identified in *Journeys Through College* was that 65% of GED passers and 56% of traditional high school graduates had a GPA of 3.0 or higher in the first year of college. Six years later (by 2009) 53% of both groups had a GPA of at least 3.25. Female, White, or older students with GED credentials tended to have higher first-year GPAs.

Nearly 90% of students from either background group expressed satisfaction with the quality of their college education. The 2009 employment rates for college students from the BPS study were 70% for GED passers and 80% for traditional high school graduates, regardless of whether they graduated from college. For both backgrounds, students who graduated from college and younger students had higher employment rates than nongraduates and older students. More than three-fifths of traditional high school graduates and half of GED passers indicated that their job was related to their college major, and between 50% and 70% of those surveyed indicated that they were satisfied with various aspects of their jobs, regardless of educational background (Guison-Dowdy & Patterson, 2011b).

With so many commonalities and so much potential for success, a critical question remains: Why is the graduation rate for adults with GED credentials so low? One piece of the answer may lie in the gradual approach adults take to completing a college education, as noted earlier; that is, a large proportion simply has yet to graduate and continues to work toward postsecondary goals (Patterson et al., 2010). Another piece may reflect the financial situation of many adults with GED credentials: As independent adults, frequently with low-paying jobs and children to support, they struggle to afford college and even get less financial aid than their classmates with traditional diplomas. The authors of *Journeys Through College* concluded with the following recommendations to support those who are at risk of not completing college programs:

> Personal situations and financial struggles . . ., rather than academic problems, that enrollees experienced after first enrolling seemed at the core of leaving the postsecondary system for both GED® test passers and traditional high school graduates. Colleges serving GED test passers need to offer ample information, guidance, and support programs geared toward the realities of GED test passers' lives . . . and the very real risk they face of leaving with no degree. (Guison-Dowdy & Patterson, 2011b, p. 27)

Perceptions and Pathways Study

Still, the available research has not fully addressed the critical question, Why is the college graduation rate among adults with GED credentials low? Following both the *Crossing the Bridge* study and the BPS analyses in *Journeys Through College*, a need to more fully explain what was happening to GED passers in college was apparent (Quigley et al., 2011). Therefore, asking adults with GED credentials to describe their educational journey from secondary through postsecondary education seemed necessary; as a result, the *Perceptions and Pathways* study ensued. In a preliminary report, the authors described how the *Perceptions and Pathways* study came about:

> The 2011 *Perceptions and Pathways* study extended [American Council on Education's] earlier research by posing the question: What experiences, motivations, and developed perceptions have influenced members of the [GED

passer] population to either choose or not choose to pursue a postsecondary education? Further, what experiences, motivations, and developed perceptions influenced those who decided not to complete postsecondary programs? The *Perceptions and Pathways* study constituted the first nationwide follow-up study of GED® test credential recipients conducted to explore such major questions. At the time of writing, a total of 85 interviews (including 10 pilot interviews) had been completed. (Quigley et al., 2011, p. 2)

Researchers envisioned four phases of an educational journey from secondary through postsecondary experiences: "1) Deciding to drop out of [high] school; 2) Deciding to take the GED test; 3) Deciding to go on to postsecondary education or not; 4) Deciding to complete postsecondary education or to drop/stop out" (Quigley et al., 2011, p. 3). Adults who had passed the GED test approximately five years earlier were selected through stratified random sampling. In-depth interviews (beginning with participants drawing a life map of their educational journey and lasting approximately one to two hours) with adults took place in six states representing "diverse geographic regions, primary adult education program type, and statewide postsecondary enrollment rates" (Quigley et al., 2011, p. 5). The six states were California, Connecticut, Kansas, North Carolina, Texas, and Wyoming, with West Virginia as a pilot state. Once states and locations were determined, adults were selected at random from within groups reflecting age, gender, and ethnic diversity.

Interviewee Perceptions About College

After identifying and coding more than 70 themes in summer 2011, researchers at ACE ceased work on *Perceptions and Pathways* because the research department was closed in September 2011. A preliminary report was published in October 2011. A number of themes and initial impressions about the role of GED testing in interviewees' futures and the environment they experienced in college were identified in that report:

> Did their future change with the GED® test? One interviewee was very clear: "I felt like I could conquer the world at that time. I felt like it was mine to take." Asked about the extent to which the GED® test credential impacted their decision to take the next step towards [postsecondary education] or a career, interviewees . . . see the GED® test credential as not only the "ticket" but the impetus to move on to postsecondary education. (Quigley et al., 2011, p. 10)

It appears that many who did go on to further education may have found the postsecondary environment completely unlike that in their past schools. While they often lacked close connections with their college instructors or counselors, some described a sense of freedom and level of respect not experienced back in secondary school. . . . Rather, some seem to feel the college or university personnel may be truly differ[ent] from past schooling personnel. (Quigley et al., 2011, p. 12)

The authors found that "the decision to go to postsecondary education may not be a capricious one, rather a step taken with high expectations and definite commitment" (Quigley et al., 2011, p. 12). The resilience of college students with GED credentials and college graduates' enthusiasm for even more postsecondary education also struck the *Perceptions and Pathways* interviewers:

> Many interviewees described their experiences in postsecondary education as positive, whether they completed or not. . . . Those who are resilient may also be diligent—more than one interviewee described working full time while attending postsecondary education full time. . . . It seems that many who leave postsecondary education are, as they see it, only stopping out. Few would say they have irrevocably quit college. Rather, returning later seems more likely. Likewise, most who have completed their programs intend to return for further study. . . . As one participant said: "I'm going to keep going [for another degree]. I'm going to keep going. I'm not going to stop here." (Quigley et al., 2011, p. 12)

Initial Perceptions and Pathways *Recommendations to College Staff*

Perceptions and Pathways interviewees made many recommendations to college staff and administrators on the basis of their postsecondary experiences. Some believed clear information on local colleges would be beneficial, even before taking the GED test. This information could include "'front-end' information and counseling in postsecondary institutions" (Quigley et al., 2011, p. 13). Quigley et al. (2011) cited an interviewee who wanted colleges to acknowledge GED passers as nontraditional students:

> I think it's better served if you really understand if a person is coming in with a nontraditional background, in the sense that they've not [been] shepherded right out of high school and kind of coached into going to school, that their experience is going to be different. I think if this interview process . . . is going to help, [it] is [for staff to realize] that . . . people that are going through a GED® [testing] program . . . may not have the traditional things that one would expect from a traditional student, because they're not traditional students. (p. 13)

One qualitative difference that set GED passers apart as nontraditional was a genuine need for encouragement from college staff, especially counselors and support staff. Some college students who passed the GED test reported encouraging themselves through college and yearning for ongoing motivation to continue. The authors cited one interviewee recommendation and pointed to GED passers' need for postsecondary supports:

> "Be more flexible and accommodate people's different life situations." Many who have gone on to postsecondary education in this study seem to indicate they had little contact with counselors or support services in postsecondary education. Further analysis would help investigate if this is a "pattern of formal institutional alienation" among college students with GED® test credentials. Deeper examination of the extent to which GED® test credential recipients choose to make use of postsecondary supports may help postsecondary retention rates. (Quigley et al., 2011, p. 13)

The interviewees also described a need for financial support and resources to begin and complete college. The authors recommended that "further examination of the financial barriers, specifically, that this group faces compared to the postsecondary mainstream would be most helpful" (Quigley et al., 2011, p. 13), particularly grants and scholarships:

> While many returning adults need financial aid, lost time and lost income are frequently the added burdens interviewees carry into the postsecondary setting. If more financial aid were available and directed to this huge group entering the postsecondary world, would completion rates rise? (p. 13)

The preliminary report concluded by indicating a few signals, such as poor attendance and low grades, that interviewees gave before they stopped out. Quigley et al. (2011) recommended further investigation of all the warning signs and interviewee recommendations that might positively affect retention.

Further Recommendations to College Staff

Quigley et al.'s (2011) report, although informative as to the scope of the project and initial impressions, was unable to fully tap into the rich set of recommendations that interviewees had made in the *Perceptions and Pathways* study. To honor the commitment researchers had made to interviewees to pass along their insights and recommendations, the former research team leader requested and gained access to *Perceptions and Pathways* data from GED Testing Service®, and in-depth analysis of interviewee data began. The following sections discuss some of the recommendations they made to community college administrators and staff who consider how to reach this vast subpopulation. One of the first sets of recommendations to postsecondary educators was presented in

November 2011 at the National College Transition Network conference and included responses from 55 interviewees (Patterson, 2011).

Interviewees gave their reactions to how colleges caught their attention and recruited them. Initially a substantial proportion of potential students with GED credentials looked online at college websites. "Anybody can get on the website and Google," commented one interviewee. Another added, "And the computer is a wonderful thing. You go to a search bar, you put in 'college' and you get endless—*endless* information about college. You can do anything" (Patterson, 2011).

Direct Contact
While many interviewees responded to information they found on websites, direct contact, such as through public college fairs or presence at community events, held additional appeal. One interviewee explained,

> I think [community colleges] *do* do a pretty good job at getting most of the information out there. Like you said, there's the [I]nternet for people. I mean I've been to the mall before when they have all the different college[s]. They have stands set up, you know? You can go there and get information. And they'll talk to you, you know. I think that's good. Maybe they could put their information more out there in public places, as well. (Patterson, 2011)

Community college administrators could also consider making special offers that would appeal to GED passers. An interviewee responded to a college's special offer and recommended that direct contact with college staff would be beneficial to other GED passers. This interviewee complimented the local college not only on outreach efforts but on going the extra mile to help students reach goals. The interviewee advised,

> You should go directly to [the college]. They are there to help people. It's more of a community or a village. You help them no matter how long it takes. You also offer a program that offers a free semester when you graduate a class and if you can express that, I think more people will join. The people here [at the college] helped me get to my goals. It opens doors for people. I think you are all doing a great job. (Patterson, 2011)

Direct contact could even extend as far as reaching out to potential college students in person. This would be especially beneficial for those GED passers who are not Internet savvy. One creative outreach idea from an interviewee, who did not know how to go about getting information from the college itself, was for the college to get the word out by going directly to GED passers at home:

I would go for it [college], but I don't know how. I think there is a lack of education on keeping people in school round here. People come knock on my door, "Will you vote for me," "Will you come to my church." I've never had anyone knock on my door and say, "Would you be interested in going to school or college?" I've never had anyone do that. They just don't pass the word around. If you want to know any information, you've got to come here and ask somebody. "Do you have any literature on going to college?" (Patterson, 2011)

Reaching Out Through Print

Many interviewees reported responding to college outreach via printed materials such as brochures and flyers. Brochures providing basic information and referring GED passers to counselors encouraged them to visit campus and get more details. A personal touch was not simply creating a brochure and disseminating it locally, but sending it directly to the GED passer, perhaps multiple times. According to one interviewee:

Before I even went there [to the college], they keep sending brochures to your homes. Once you live in the neighborhood, they just drop a flyer in the mail. They'll tell you, "If you have GED [credential], high school diploma, or whatever, feel free to come in. We have counseling people." They do, to me, a pretty good job. My advice would be continue whatever they could do to improve, maybe hold public sessions, whatever. (Patterson, 2011)

Another GED passer saw a connection between outreach via print materials and data on college majors or career fields that most appeal to GED passers. This interviewee recommended,

I would say maybe have brochures. Maybe reach out to certain, for example, fields. What kinds of fields are more appealing to students who graduated [with] the GED [credential]? Or maybe ask in the middle of the course, "What would you like to do after this? What was a life dream?" Something that's reachable and is there courses out there for them that they can take and better themselves. (Patterson, 2011)

Another interviewee made a connection between outreach via print and searching online:

Yeah, free ads in the mail. I am one of the persons, the mail comes and I check everything. So if there is something that interests me or something that I want to be into, just information. And also, of course, the desire to do certain things so you search for the way or you will find the way. To see the information first and then you search. (Patterson, 2011)

Colleges could also reach out to GED passers where they spend the most time and would be most likely to read print materials. Places where adults have to wait, such as doctors' offices or pharmacies, would be prime locations for these materials, according to one interviewee:

> There again, it's all going to be basically down to the literature that you have. . . . I know I do a lot of reading when I'm waiting on my medication at the drug stores. . . . Sometimes you are in there a good hour. . . . If you just got to look over and see a pamphlet or something and say, "Let me read that." A lot of people will read something even though they don't read at home or whatever. They'll pick something up just to occupy their mind while they are waiting on their medication. . . . I think so. Doctors' offices. You are waiting for your appointment. Different places like that. (Patterson, 2011)

Other Forms of Outreach

Some interviewees with GED credentials advised the use of media such as newspapers, magazines, television, radio, and even billboards. As with the other forms of outreach just described, some GED passers preferred responding to special offers, such as appeals to adult career interests or student discounts to sporting events. Five specific suggestions follow (Patterson, 2011):

1. "Advertise it on television or radio. People will always listen to that. They may not listen to the same music I listen to, but they listen to the radio. You know, announcements, public announcements."
2. "Newspaper, magazines [in Spanish]. . . . Just like I [am] saying, television, newspapers because everybody reads in Spanish or another language."
3. "On TV. You see the commercials. . . . The only thing that I find wrong is that [TV ads for college] make it sound too easy, because it's not easy. It's a two year course crammed into nine months."
4. "Probably showing a TV commercial of . . . what I would like to do, and say, 'With the help of this college, this is how I do this,' or something like that. You just can't sell a bunch of kids sitting around all bored, like they're not having a good time. It's got to catch your eye somehow."
5. "Maybe a billboard. You see billboards everywhere, all these lights and stuff. 'Now you can save on GEICO insurance.' But it doesn't say anything about, 'Interested about going back to school? Call us,' or anything like that. . . . I might go just so I can get a student discount on tickets for sports. . . . It's a good way to advertise. You can show a team

playing basketball, and say, 'For five dollars you could see this. Call for a five-dollar ticket.' And then it's, 'Well, these are student prices. We'd like to get you enrolled in school.' Whereas you would pay $85 to see the same game. Stuff like that is what catches my eye. What are they going to do at the college besides study all the time?"

Recommendations About College Counseling

In the *Perceptions and Pathways* interviews, adults with GED credentials were frank about their experiences with college counseling and generally described counselors and the guidance they received in a positive light. One interviewee urged GED passers:

> Go talk to a community college counselor. They'll be able to kind of point you into the right direction. . . . If you don't know what to do or where you're going, call them. You can call the desk and they'll tell you. "Here's the best way you can do this. You can come talk to one of our counselors. Set up an appointment or you just come in." They'll point you to where you would like to be. (Patterson, 2011)

Some interviewees were convinced that counseling is even more than helping them to select courses or search for financial aid. GED passers indicated needing counselors to help them think through future career paths, select a college, and take college entrance exams. "I think [supporting people is] helping to guide their process in finding where they want to be and finding which colleges are best for them," said one interviewee. Another stated, "I don't think that I would have felt comfortable taking it [the SAT test]. They could say, 'Come and talk to our counselors [about testing]'" (Patterson, 2011).

Recommendations on Financial Aid

Because much of the GED testing target population lives in poverty (GED Testing Service, 2010) and many adults rely on scholarships to cover the costs of the GED test, GED passers saw college cost as one of the most challenging and frightening aspects of attending college. The fear appears to stem both from lack of money and from lack of experience in how to access money for college. "It's kind of scary when they talk about financial aid," related an interviewee. "They really stress how a lot of people don't qualify for financial aid or get enough grants. It freaks people out. Once you start talking that, they kind of shy away from it. . . . Because the money is the one thing that scares people from college. It's really expensive" (Patterson, 2011).

Another interviewee agreed about the need for guidance on financial aid and added that counselors could provide the guidance needed to help GED passers navigate through the system to get financial aid. "Most of [GED passers] all need some kind of financial help, now-a-days. I'm sure that if they're thinking about going back to school, then there's counselors here at the college that can say, 'Oh. We have grants or students loans'" (Patterson, 2011).

When asked specifically how counselors could help adults with GED credentials navigate through financial aid, an interviewee saw a need for colleges to explicitly offer information in a publicly accessible place:

> [They could], say, advertise somehow, "Come to the school and let us help you get started." . . . There's so many scholarships out there that's available that nobody knows about them. . . . I think somewhere in a college there should be a room with everything posted on it, instead of in somebody's mind or in a book that's on somebody's desk and unless you ask, they don't tell. It should be posted. Or a computer that you can go to a college computer in the library and you go look up scholarships. Let them know that it's there. In the classroom, somewhere. Say, "Hey. This is available for you." (Patterson, 2011)

Knowing what to access, where to access it, and how to access the information would have helped this interviewee with identifying and applying for college scholarships. Other interviewees want information and guidance about financial aid before making the decision to go to college. They required it at the time of GED testing, as they considered options for what was next in their lives. One interviewee saw getting timely information about financial aid as life transforming:

> I know you guys have all these peoples' names that have gotten their GED [credential]s. I would be sending those people some types of mail. Some type of flyer. Some type of whatever's the best, cheapest investment for sending out however many you would need to inform people that college is possible with financial aid, if you don't have it. These are the courses and classes we offer. Because once people get that information in their hand, then everything changes. I mean, my world was changed once I had that information. "Oh, okay. I can do this now." All of it changes. (Patterson, 2011)

Another interviewee saw information about how to afford community college as critical to making the decision to go. This interviewee recommended direct outreach to GED credential recipients:

> If you have their addresses—the people that graduate [with GED credentials]—I would send them information or a pamphlet or something on grant money, on financial aid, to come to [XXX Community College].

Part time or full time if they can. Because I didn't know about it until somebody told me. . . . A lot of people, if they knew they could get financial aid, they would go to college. (Patterson, 2011)

GED passers with children had specific suggestions related to child care and housing for adult students on campus, as well as student employment. One interviewee with children recommended,

If colleges could offer the daycare or family housing, or even if they just discounted it and added it to the student loans [it would help]. I'm also looking into student loans, so I was thinking of trying to get enough student loans to help me go to school and pay bills, so that I would only need to work part-time. Just add that into the whole student loan process. I could pay it back after and not be trying to pay for daycare and everything while I'm going to school. Just add it to the loan and pay it later. That would help. And if all of them had the family housing option, it would be a lot easier and cheaper to live on campus. . . . Maybe special jobs on campus . . . Just make sure they have lots of jobs like that open to students, part-time. (Patterson, 2011)

Recommendations From GED Passers With Special Needs

The latest report employing *Perceptions and Pathways* interviewee data focused on the experiences and recommendations of GED passers with disabilities, chronic health issues, and other special needs. College enrollees with special needs who had passed the GED test reported benefiting from a number of transitional supports (Patterson, in press). Some of these supports were financial, as noted in the preliminary report and later findings (Patterson, 2011; Quigley et al., 2011). In addition to a need for information on financial aid before starting a college program, interviewees indicated a need for assurances that they could get a job in their major after graduation. They needed financial support not only for tuition costs but also for textbooks and child care. Several interviewees indicated they needed to go to college in a convenient location so that transportation would not be a barrier (Patterson, in press).

Managing their college schedule around the rest of their life was a need for several interviewees with special needs. They talked about needing a "manageable schedule" and flexible class times. Some advocated for a step-by-step approach to completing college. One young male enrollee suggested that if "life is too hectic, find something that is better prepared, or on your schedule. . . . Right now, we're moving into an age where things are now, they're working around our schedules" (Patterson, in press). A middle-aged female interviewee advised,

> My advice is just to take as much as you can at once. Don't get discouraged and just keep going. Some people can take one or two [classes]. I would need to take one class, just to be able to handle it, but some people can take a lot of classes. I would say, "Don't worry about time because you got all the time in the world. Just get it done." (Patterson, in press)

In addition to offering responsive scheduling, community college staff could actively promote counseling services. Interviewees with special needs who did not take advantage of counseling services sometimes lacked information on how to even get counseling. As one young female interviewee admitted, "The counselor might have helped if I went to them but I didn't know who to go to or where to go" (Patterson, in press).

Additional helpful transitional supports that interviewees suggested were required early counseling and a first-semester course to acclimate students to college requirements. A young male interviewee recommended,

> I think the college provides classes [to find your way]. I remember in my first semester, they had the classes where you had to go and write down certain things about memorable items. Like, you know, go to the library and pick something up and prove that you went to the library and you know where the library is. . . . One of the classes was background research about the history of the college. About different parts of the building. And I thought that class was wonderful, and for anybody coming in, because it *forced* you to get out and see what was available, to *see* what the options were. So I think that's really good for, as far as a prerequisite or a requirement, to take the classes. The counselor, I think is equally as influential. I would go as far to say that . . . you have to meet with the counselor at least once or twice or three times throughout your first semester. . . . A student should be closer to somebody with the information to be able to provide a direction for that student. (Patterson, in press)

Conclusion

According to *Crossing the Bridge* research (Patterson et al., 2010; Zhang et al., 2011), 43% of GED passers enroll in postsecondary education within six years of testing. This percentage is important because it estimates the extent to which GED passers, a major alternative group of high school completers, go to college. *Crossing the Bridge* postsecondary enrollees tended to be young and female. Ethnically, one in six was either African American or Hispanic, and an estimated three in five enrollees were White. Most adults with GED credentials enrolled within three years of testing, with peak enrollment at 14–15 months after testing. Although GED passers may need some time to make the decision to go to college and to actually enroll, they tend not to delay entry very long.

Approximately 1 of every 12 entering first-year college students has GED credentials. The vast majority of GED passers enroll in community colleges (Patterson, 2010; Patterson et al., 2010; Zhang et al., 2011). Reports indicate that 100,000 or more GED passers per cohort year could be expected to flow into community colleges across the United States. The graduation rate for GED-passer postsecondary enrollees (12%) in both cohorts was very low. About 62% overall dropped out. In the 2003 cohort of GED passers, female, White, or older students who attended college programs of two years or less had higher odds of graduating from community college, as did students who completed 12th grade and those who enrolled full-time (Patterson, 2010).

Persistence may also be related to increasing levels of educational experience (R-Ally™, 2012). GED passers may experience education gradually, sometimes even step by step, as they gain educational maturity. GED passers appear to need extended time. Enrolling at least 8 semesters may serve as a tipping point for persistence. Nearly half of GED passers enrolling for 8–14 semesters graduated.

A key message from *Journeys Through College* is that adults with GED credentials, though generally older and more financially independent, are surprisingly similar to traditional high school graduates in many fundamental ways. Regardless of educational background, most college enrollees were female, and a large proportion went to community colleges. For both groups the primary reason for entering college was to secure a steady job. A majority of GED passers and traditional high school graduates attended college full-time. A common need is for financial aid; approximately 85% of either group applied for this financial assistance. On average, however, adults with GED credentials received approximately 25% less in financial aid than their counterparts (Guison-Dowdy & Patterson, 2011b).

Unexpectedly, it was found that approximately 21% of first-year college students—from either background—took developmental coursework. Another similarity was in college GPA; by 2009, 53% of both groups had a GPA of at least 3.25. Female, White, or older students with GED credentials tended to have higher GPAs. The 2009 employment rates were high for both groups, regardless of whether they graduated from college or not.

With so many similarities and so much potential for success, an important question remains: Why is the graduation rate for adults with GED credentials so low? One possible factor may be the gradual approach adults take to completing a college education. Another possible factor may be that GED passers frequently have low-paying jobs and children to support and are unable to get as much financial aid as those with traditional diplomas, making it difficult to afford college (Guison-Dowdy & Patterson, 2011b).

To more fully explain persistence in college, the *Perceptions and Pathways* qualitative study asked adults with GED credentials to describe their educational journey from secondary through postsecondary education. *Perceptions and Pathways* interviewees made many recommendations to college staff and administrators on the basis of their postsecondary experiences. Some stated that clear information on local colleges and counseling would be beneficial, even before taking the GED test (Quigley et al., 2011).

Interviewees reacted to how colleges caught their attention. Initially a substantial proportion of potential students with GED credentials looked online at college websites. Although many interviewees responded to information they found on websites, direct contact, such as through public college fairs or presence at community events, held additional appeal. Direct contact could even extend as far as reaching out to potential college students at home, especially because not all GED passers are Internet savvy, or in places where adults have to wait, such as doctors' offices (Patterson, 2011).

In the *Perceptions and Pathways* interviews, adults generally described college counselors and the guidance they received in a positive light. GED passers indicated needing counselors to help them think through future career paths, select a college, and take entrance exams. Counselors could also provide the guidance needed to help GED passers navigate through the system to get financial aid. Knowing what to access, where to access it, and how to access the information would have helped interviewees with identifying and applying for college scholarships. GED passers with children had specific suggestions regarding child care, housing for adult students on campus, and student employment (Patterson, 2011).

College enrollees with special needs who had passed the GED test indicated a need for assurances that they could get a job in their major after graduation. They needed financial support for tuition costs as well as textbooks and child care. Several interviewees required a convenient college location so that transportation would not be a barrier. College staff could focus on providing easy access to accurate and complete information, such as on the accessibility and convenience of branch locations or the availability of transportation resources (Patterson, in press).

Being able to manage their college schedule around the rest of their life and having flexible class times were needs for several interviewees with special needs. Additional helpful transitional supports were required early counseling and a first-semester course to acclimate students to college requirements. Interviewees with special needs who did not take advantage of counseling services sometimes lacked information on how to even get counseling.

Outreach efforts—such as college tours, open houses, or first-semester orientations—need to be explicit and offer concrete solutions to challenges adults face while making college decisions. In an era of widespread technology use, getting college access and decision-making information should not be a mystifying or secretive process for adults; rather, information about getting to the college, getting financial aid, identifying a counselor, and other common challenges should be transparent and publicly accessible (Patterson, in press). College staff can also work with adult educators to refer transitioning learners to first-semester college acclimation programs, outreach tours, and intake counseling at local colleges.

This chapter has described a major yet often invisible population of adult learners, an untapped resource with vast potential. One in eight entering students has a GED credential, along with bright prospects and hopes for a new career and family-supporting wages. Community college staff and administrators can unlock that potential as they learn from research findings on GED passers and interviewee insights and recommendations—and apply the results as enhancements to service and outreach.

References

Aud, S., KewalRamani, A., & Frohlich, L. (2011). *America's youth: Transitions to adulthood* (NCES 2012-026). Washington, DC: U.S. Department of Education, National Center for Education Statistics.

Bound, J., Lovenheim, M., & Turner, S. (2010). *Increasing time to baccalaureate degree in the United States.* NBER Working Paper 15892. Cambridge, MA: National Bureau of Economic Research.

Crissey, S., & Bauman, K. (2012). *Measurement of high school equivalency credentials in Census Bureau surveys.* SEHSD Working Paper No. 2012-3. Washington, DC: U.S. Census Bureau.

GED Testing Service. (2010). *2009 GED testing program statistical report.* Washington, DC: American Council on Education. Available at www.gedtestingservice.com

GED Testing Service. (2012). *2011 GED testing program statistical report.* Washington, DC: American Council on Education. Available at www.gedtestingservice.com

Guison-Dowdy, A., & Patterson, M. B. (2011a). *Journeys through college: Postsecondary transitions and outcomes of GED® test passers.* Washington, DC: American Council on Education. Available at www.gedtestingservice.com

Guison-Dowdy, A., & Patterson, M. B. (2011b). *Journeys through college 2: Postsecondary experiences of GED® test passers.* Washington, DC: American Council on Education. Available at www.gedtestingservice.com

Horn, L. (2010). *Tracking students to 200 percent of normal time: Effect on institutional graduation rates* (NCES 2011-221). Washington, DC: National Center for Education Statistics.

Patterson, M. B. (2010). *GED® test passers in postsecondary institutions of up to two years: Following up on enrollment and graduation.* Washington, DC: American Council on Education, GED Testing Service.

Patterson, M. B. (2011). In their own words: GED® credential recipients share recommendations for postsecondary and adult educators. In *Life experiences from GED credential to college: Perceptions and pathways.* PowerPoint presentation at National College Transition Network annual conference, Warwick, RI.

Patterson, M. B. (in press). *Post-GED-credential college prospects for adults with special needs.*

Patterson, M. B., Zhang, J., Song, W., & Guison-Dowdy, A. (2010). *Crossing the bridge: GED credentials and postsecondary outcomes (Year 1 report).* Washington, DC: American Council on Education. Available at www.gedtestingservice.com

Quigley, B. A., Patterson, M. B., & Zhang, J. (2011). *Perceptions and pathways: Decisions of GED test credential recipients from secondary to postsecondary education—A preliminary report.* Washington, DC: American Council on Education. Available at www.gedtestingservice.com

R-Ally™: Research Allies for Lifelong Learning. (2012). Retrieved from www .researchallies.org

Reder, S. (2007). *Adult education and postsecondary success.* New York, NY: Council for Advancement of Adult Literacy. Retrieved from www.nationalcommissionon adultliteracy.org/content/rederpolicybriefrev10807.pdf

Zhang, J., Guison-Dowdy, A., Patterson, M. B., & Song, W. (2011). *Crossing the bridge: GED credentials and postsecondary educational outcomes: Year two report.* Washington, DC: American Council on Education.

3

FROM GED® TO POSTSECONDARY EDUCATION

The Role of Institutions

Wei Song

Keep away from people who try to belittle your ambitions. Small people always do that, but the really great make you feel that you, too, can become great.

—Mark Twain

While the United States continues to recover from an economic recession, the need for adults to be prepared for family-sustaining careers is acute for the economy as well as for individuals (Council for Advancement of Adult Literacy [CAAL], 2008; Office of Vocational and Adult Education [OVAE], 2010; Reder, 2007, 2010; Southern Regional Education Board [SREB], 2010). To reach economic stability, adults without a high school diploma need further education, not just through the adult secondary level, but beyond (Tyler & Lofstrum, 2010). The General Education Development (GED®) credential is now a significant gateway to postsecondary education (PSE; Reder, 2007). A majority of adults passing the GED test (American Council on Education [ACE], 2011) report further education as a reason for testing, and approximately 43% of GED passers eventually enroll in PSE (Patterson, Zhang, Song, & Guison-Dowdy, 2010; Zhang, Guison-Dowdy, Patterson, & Song, 2011).

What is less known about the educational pipeline for adult learners is whether there is a connection, through a GED testing center, between GED testing and PSE. More than 25% of GED testing centers are located in community colleges, which are the most frequent host agencies for GED testing, according to a recent survey of GED testing centers (GED Testing Service®, 2011; Guison-Dowdy & Patterson, 2011). As adults without high school diplomas come to these colleges to take the GED test, they may explore postsecondary programs at these colleges or receive encouragement to enroll for credit programs after GED testing. What is the role of the postsecondary institution in testing GED candidates and transitioning them to PSE? How does a postsecondary institution serve as part of an effective pipeline to transition adults without high school credentials to PSE?

More than three quarters of entering students with GED credentials initially enrolled in two-year colleges, primarily in public institutions in states where they took the GED test (Bound, Lovenheim, & Turner, 2010; Zhang et al., 2011). The relatively wide availability of adult education programs, remedial services, and flexible learning programs (such as distance-learning opportunities) at most of these institutions (Zhang et al., 2011) may help them transition into PSE. This availability is particularly key for learners with low skill levels who may ultimately struggle to persist in PSE (Reder, 2007).

The review of literature on GED test takers and postsecondary institutions just discussed has led to the following research questions to be addressed by the present study:

1. What is the percentage of GED test takers who test in test centers located in a postsecondary institution (PSE test center) in contrast to those testing in test centers at other locations (non-PSE test center)? How does test performance contrast between test takers from PSE test centers and those from non-PSE test centers?

2. What differences in PSE outcomes do GED passers who tested in PSE test centers versus in non-PSE test centers experience in terms of time to PSE enrollment, enrollment rate, time to degree, and graduation rate?

3. What percentage of GED passers testing in PSE centers later enroll in the same postsecondary institution where they tested? What are the top 100 institutions nationally that transition GED passers to their own postsecondary programs after GED testing?

4. How do institutional characteristics differ between those that transitioned a higher percentage of GED passers into their own institutions and those that transitioned a lower percentage?

Data and Methodology

For the first research question, individual-level data of more than 700,000 GED candidates were extracted from the GED Testing Service® database, which houses each GED test candidate's demographic information and test records. The percentage for the GED candidates tested through PSE centers was calculated for the year 2010, the most recent year for which testing data are available. Making multiple-year comparisons would allow for even stronger cross-validation of results; however, GED Testing Service did not collect testing center profile data for every year. In addition, from 2002 to 2010, the demographics and test performance of GED candidates were stable (ACE, 2003–2011). Thus, using the most recent data should be sufficient for the purpose of the first research question.

The mean test scores in each content area and the mean total battery scores were compared, using a *t*-test and effect size, between those who tested through PSE centers and those who tested through non-PSE centers. For effect size on mean differences, Cohen's *d* (Cohen, 1988) is used, with a minimum level of 0.30 for meaningful practical significance.

For the second research question, the postsecondary outcomes of GED passers are based on a data match of GED passers' data with National Student Clearinghouse (NSC) data at the individual level. NSC is a nonprofit organization that holds data from approximately 3,000 postsecondary institutions and currently maintains records for approximately 93% of the total U.S. postsecondary student enrollment. To allow enough time to observe GED passers' PSE experiences, the data match used a 2004 cohort of GED candidates and allowed six years (from 2004 to fall 2010) for the GED candidates to enroll in and graduate from postsecondary institutions. The match also yielded information on GED candidates' postsecondary enrollment starting and ending dates, enrollment status, attendance status (i.e., full-time or less), degrees, and majors. Comparisons are done for the PSE enrollment rate, time from passing the GED test to PSE enrollment, time to degree, and graduation rate between the GED passers who tested through PSE centers and those who tested through non-PSE centers, again testing for statistical and practical significance. For effect size on proportion comparison, Cohen's *h* is used, which has the same interpretation as Cohen's *d* in terms of scales.

For the third and fourth research questions, the GED-NSC data were matched with the 2005 Integrated Postsecondary Education Data System (IPEDS) institution data for further analyses. IPEDS is a system of interrelated surveys conducted annually by the U.S. Department of Education's National Center for Education Statistics (NCES) to gather information from every college, university, and technical and vocational institution that participates in federal financial aid programs. More than 6,700 institutions complete IPEDS surveys annually.

Through the IPEDS institution locator, the PSE GED testing centers and the postsecondary institutions reported by NSC were matched to examine whether GED passers enrolled in the same institutions where they tested. Altogether 682 GED testing centers housed in postsecondary institutions were identified. After identifying 472 postsecondary institutions that tested at least 50 GED passers who later enrolled in PSE, the institutions were ranked based on the rate at which an institution transitioned GED passers into its own postsecondary programs. This rate, calculated from the number of GED passers who enrolled at the same institution where they tested divided by the total number of the GED passers who tested at this institution and enrolled at any PSE institution, is defined as *transition rate* herein. Furthermore, the 472 institutions are divided into quartiles and used IPEDS institutional data to descriptively analyze the relationships between GED passers' PSE enrollment and institutional characteristics in the top (75th percentile and above) and bottom (25th percentile and below) quartiles, such as sector, location, services, and programs.

GED Testing Through PSE Centers and Test Performance

Postsecondary institutions are a major channel for adults not completing high school to earn a GED credential. In 2010, 30% of GED testing centers in the United States were located in a postsecondary institution (26% in community colleges and 4% in four-year institutions). These institutions tested 44% of all GED candidates. In addition, many GED testing centers are located in adult education centers (nearly 20%) and career or technical centers (approximately 7%), and some of these centers may be co-located with postsecondary institutions. Because they were not reported primarily as postsecondary sites, the testing centers designated as adult education, career, or technical centers are not included as "PSE centers" in the analyses.

Table 3.1 presents the average GED test performance of GED candidates who tested in PSE centers and those who tested in non-PSE centers. The statistics show that GED candidates who tested through PSE centers had test scores in each content area higher than those of their peers who tested through non-PSE centers. Although these differences are statistically significant, the very small effect sizes indicate these differences had no practical significance and may simply be an artifact of the large sample size.

PSE Enrollment and Persistence Patterns

Table 3.2 presents postsecondary outcomes of GED passers by type of testing center when they took the GED test. GED passers who tested at PSE centers

TABLE 3.1
GED Candidates' Test Performance by Testing Center Type: 2010

Content Area	Mean Standard Score of Candidates Tested		t-test (P > |t|)	Effect Size (Cohen's d)
	PSE Centers	Non-PSE Centers		
Writing	489	481	<0.001	0.10
Social studies	512	508	<0.001	0.05
Science	515	509	<0.001	0.07
Reading	540	535	<0.001	0.05
Mathematics	477	472	<0.001	0.06
Total score (passers only)	2,636	2,613	<0.001	0.08

Note. The number of GED test takers varied by content area because not all candidates completed the GED test. Overall, approximately 240,000 candidates tested in PSE centers and 310,000 tested in non-PSE centers in each content area. Among the passers, about 190,000 tested in PSE centers and 250,000 tested in non-PSE centers.
Source. GED Testing Service 2010 data.

TABLE 3.2
Postsecondary Outcomes of GED Passers by Testing Center Type: 2004 Cohort

	GED Passers Tested		t-test[a] (P < |t|)	Effect Size (Cohen's h)[b]
	PSE Centers	Non-PSE Centers		
Enrollment				
PSE enrollment rate (%)	47.0	40.1	<0.001	0.14
Time to enrollment (months)	22.3	24.6	<0.001	−0.05
Graduation				
Graduation rate (%)	13.1	10.9	<0.001	0.07
Type of first postsecondary credential earned				
Certificate (%)	44.9	28.8	<0.001	0.34
Associate (%)	34.5	48.0	<0.001	−0.28
Bachelor (%)	19.8	21.8	0.241	—

(Continues)

TABLE 3.2 (Cont.)

| | GED Passers Tested | | | |
	PSE Centers	Non-PSE Centers	t-test[a] (P < |t|)	Effect Size (Cohen's h)[b]
Time to first credential (months)[c]				
Certificate	17.2	17.9	0.098	—
Associate	34.3	34.8	0.165	—

Note. For enrollment rate, N = 172,263 for PSE centers and N = 222,011 for non-PSE centers; for graduation rate, N = 81,010 for PSE centers and N = 89,021 for non-PSE centers; for degrees reported, N = 7,817 for PSE centers and N = 7,426 for non-PSE centers.
[a]Chi square test for proportions.
[b]Effect size was not calculated for statistically insignificant differences.
[c]Time to bachelor's degree could not be reported by testing center type because of inconsistent reporting of enrollment dates for the small proportion of graduates with bachelor's degrees.

enrolled in PSE at a nominally higher rate (47% versus 40%) than their peers who tested in non-PSE centers, but at a practical level the differences are not significant. GED passers who tested through PSE centers enrolled at about the same time (22 months versus 25 months) as those who tested at non-PSE centers after they passed the GED test. The graduation rate is also comparable (13% versus 11%) for GED passers who tested at PSE and non-PSE centers.

In terms of first postsecondary credential obtained after they enrolled in PSE, 45% of GED passers who tested through PSE centers obtained a postsecondary certificate, 35% earned an associate's degree, and 20% received a bachelor's degree. In contrast, 29% of GED passers who tested through non-PSE centers earned a postsecondary certificate; almost half (48%) earned an associate's degree as their first PSE credential. This significant finding suggests that GED candidates who tested at PSE centers may have somewhat different postsecondary plans and experiences from those testing at non-PSE centers.

Time to degree was about the same for both groups of GED passers: more than 17 months to earn a certificate and more than 34 months for an associate's degree.

GED Passers Who Tested in PSE Centers Enrolling in the Same Institution

For the 2004 cohort of GED passers who tested at a PSE test center and then later enrolled in PSE, 52% chose the institution where they took the GED test to start their PSE, and 48% chose a different institution. In other words, postsecondary institutions with a GED test center on site were able to transfer 52% of the GED passers who eventually enrolled in PSE into their own institutions. For better elaboration, the rate of GED passers who enrolled at the same institution where they tested divided by the total number of the GED passers who tested at that institution and enrolled at any PSE institution is defined as *transition rate*.

Transition rate differs across different types of postsecondary institutions. Almost all GED passers who tested at PSE centers tested in two sectors of the PSE institutions: public two-year institutions (87%) and public four-year institutions (12%). Fifty-seven percent of GED passers who tested at a two-year public institution (e.g., a community college) chose to enroll at the same institution when they started PSE education, whereas only 27% of the GED passers who tested at public four-year institutions chose to do so.

Is enrolling at the same institution relevant to the enrollees' postsecondary experiences? Table 3.3 presents comparisons on selected PSE outcomes between the GED passers who chose to enroll at the same postsecondary institution where they took the GED test and those who tested in one postsecondary institution and chose to enroll at another.

TABLE 3.3
Postsecondary Outcomes of GED Passers by Whether Enrolling at the Same Institution of Testing: 2004 Cohort

| | GED Passers Enrolled | | | |
	Same Institution	Different Institution	t-test[a] (P < |t|)	Effect Size (Cohen's h)[b]
Time to enrollment (months)	17.3	27.2	<0.001	0.46
Graduation rate (%)	13.6	12.7	<0.002	−0.03
Time to first credential (months)[c]				
Certificate	19.3	14.4	<0.001	−0.33
Associate	36.0	31.5	<0.001	−0.30

Note. For time to enrollment and graduation rate, $N = 41,408$ for same-institution enrollees and $N = 37,544$ for different-institution enrollees; for certificates, $N = 1,863$ for same institution enrollees and $N = 1,121$ for different-institution enrollees; for associate's degrees, $N = 1,452$ for same-institution enrollees and $N = 950$ for different-institution enrollees.
[a]Chi square test for proportions.
[b]Effect size was not calculated for statistically insignificant differences.
[c]Time to bachelor's degree could not be reported by testing center type because of inconsistent reporting of enrollment dates for the small proportion of graduates with bachelor's degrees.

As shown in Table 3.3, on average, GED passers who enrolled at the same institution where they tested began their PSE programs much sooner (about 10 months earlier) than those who chose to enroll at a different institution. This difference is both statistically significant and practically significant; the effect size is medium in scale.

In terms of graduation, the rate was about the same for both groups. Regarding time to first credential, on average, those who enrolled at a different institution earned their certificate or associate's degree four to five months sooner than those who enrolled at the same institution. These differences are statistically significant and have a small effect size.

Still, statistics in Table 3.3 show that postsecondary institutions transitioning GED passers to their own PSE programs may help GED passers to gain an advantageous position in terms of early enrollment and early graduation. Even though it took these GED passers longer to earn their degrees, because they tended to enroll much earlier, their graduation dates were still months earlier than those who waited longer to enroll at different institutions. Therefore, it is important and informative to examine further the transition rate at institution level.

The transition rate varied substantially across institutions—it can range from zero to >95%. To make a meaningful ranking of the PSE institutions by transition rate, only those institutions that tested at least 50 GED passers who later enrolled in PSE were selected. Of the 682 postsecondary institutions, there were 472 that tested 50 or more GED passers who enrolled in PSE.

A top 100 list, representing a transition rate of greater than 72% from GED testing to postsecondary enrollment in the same institution for the 2004 GED passer cohort, approximating the upper quartile for transition rate, is presented in the appendix. On this list, the single college enrolling the highest number of GED passers was Portland Community College in Portland, Oregon, which enrolled 673 of its 777 GED passers in the 2004 cohort. The single college with the highest transition rate, 95%, was San Juan College in Farmington, New Mexico, which enrolled 170 of its 179 GED passers who enrolled in any PSE programs.

A closer look at the states listed in the appendix reveals that slightly more than half of U.S. states are represented, indicating widespread geographic dispersion of transition rates. Twenty-nine states had colleges or universities with high transition rates in the top 100 list, and most of these states were concentrated in the southern or western regions of the United States. States with the highest number of colleges or universities in the top 100 were North Carolina, with 12 colleges; Illinois, with 11 colleges; and Washington, with 8 colleges. Among the top 100 institutions that have the highest transition rates, 37% were in the Southeast, 18% in the Great

Lakes, 16% in the Far West, and 11% in the Southwest. Eight percent were in the Plains, 6% in the Rocky Mountains, 3% in New England, and 1% in the Mideast.

The number of GED passers enrolling tended to be small, yet transition rates were very high for colleges of varying enrollment size. Just four colleges enrolled more than 400 GED passers into their postsecondary programs: Portland Community College (Oregon), Florida State College at Jacksonville, College of Lake County (Illinois), and College of DuPage (Illinois). Five schools had transition rates exceeding 90% (i.e., 90% or more of their GED passers enrolled in the same school): San Juan College (New Mexico), Southwestern Illinois College (Illinois), University of Alaska Anchorage (Alaska), Bellingham Technical College (Washington), and Southeast Kentucky Community and Technical College (Kentucky).

Characteristics of Postsecondary Institutions With a High Transition Rate

In the previous section, the top postsecondary institutions with high transition rates (i.e., those with a high proportion of GED passers enrolled at the same institution where they passed the GED tests) were listed. What are the characteristics of these institutions compared with those with a lower transition rate? To address this question, the institutions that had at least 50 GED passers in 2004 who later enrolled in PSE were selected. The 472 institutions were then ranked by their transition rate and divided into quartiles. By comparing the top quartile (transition rate at 71% and above) and bottom quartile (transition rate at 36% and below) of the institutions, the differences in the institution characteristics associated with transition rate can be identified.

Table 3.4 lists the geographic distribution, urbanity, and sector of the top-quartile and bottom-quartile institutions. The institutions that had a higher proportion of GED passers enrolled in PSE programs at their own institutions were more likely to be located in Great Lakes, Plains, Southeast, and Far West states, while the institutions with lower transition rates tended to be in states in the Mideast, Plains, Southeast, and Southwest. In terms of the urbanity of their location, institutions in the bottom quartile were more likely to be in midsized and large cities, while those in the top quartile tended to be in small cities as well as in rural areas.

The distribution of institution sector is very different for the top quartile and bottom quartile. The first quartile of institutions comprises predominantly public two-year institutions (97%), while only 60% of the bottom quartile of institutions included public two-year colleges, and 31% were public four-year institutions.

TABLE 3.4
**Sector and Location of Postsecondary Institutions in Top Quartile and
Bottom Quartile by Transition Rate**

	Top Quartile (%) (N = 117)	Bottom Quartile (%) (N = 119)
Geographic region[a]		
New England	3.4	0.8
Mideast	2.6	10.1
Great Lakes	17.1	7.6
Plains	10.3	17.7
Southeast	36.8	29.4
Southwest	9.4	23.5
Rocky Mountains	5.1	5.0
Far West	15.4	5.9
Urbanity		
City: large	8.6	24.4
City: midsize	5.1	13.5
City: small	17.1	10.9
Suburb: large	4.3	9.2
Suburb: midsize	3.4	0.0
Suburb: small	0.9	1.7
Town: fringe	3.4	1.7
Town: distant	9.4	6.7
Town: remote	10.3	12.6
Rural: fringe	27.4	16.0
Rural: distant	8.6	2.5
Rural: remote	1.7	0.8
Sector		
Public, 4-year or above	2.6	31.1
Private not-for-profit, 4-year or above	0.0	5.0
Private for-profit, 4-year or above	0.0	0.8

(*Continues*)

TABLE 3.4 (Cont.)

	Top Quartile (%) (N = 117)	Bottom Quartile (%) (N = 119)
Public, 2-year	97.4	59.7
Private not-for-profit, 2-year	0.0	1.7
Public, less than 2-year	0.0	1.7

Note. Percentages may not add up to 100% due to rounding.
[a]IPEDS geographic region categories are as follows: New England (CT, ME, MA, NH, RI, VT); Mideast (DE, DC, MD, NJ, NY, PA); Great Lakes (IL, IN, MI, OH, WI); Plains (IA, KS, MN, MO, NE, ND, SD); Southeast (AL, AR, FL, GA, KY, LA, MS, NC, SC, TN, VA, WV); Southwest (AZ, NM, OK, TX); Rocky Mountains (CO, ID, MT, UT, WY); Far West (AK, CA, HI, NV, OR, WA).

Table 3.5 presents the enrollment size and student demographics of the institutions in the top and bottom quartiles. The institutions in the top quartile tend to be smaller compared with those in the bottom quartile. The student age, gender, and ethnic distributions are comparable for the two groups.

Table 3.6 displays information on open admission policy, retention, and graduation rates at the institutions in the top and bottom quartiles. Almost all (97%) of the institutions in the top quartile had an open enrollment policy, compared with only 67% in the bottom quartile. This difference might provide one explanation for the higher proportion of GED passers who enrolled at the institutions in the top quartile after they tested there. The retention rate and graduation rate at the top-quartile and bottom-quartile institutions were very comparable.

Which services postsecondary institutions provide for GED passers may also play an important role in transitioning to PSE programs. GED passers tend to be older, have left school longer, and have more family responsibilities than traditional PSE enrollees; thus, they may need more support or services at postsecondary institutions.

Table 3.7 presents information on selected student services and support at the institutions in the top and bottom quartiles. Institutions in the top quartile led those in the bottom quartile in terms of services and special programs provided, particularly in on-campus day care, occupational education, and adult basic remedial services; in these areas the percentages of the institutions in the top quartile providing such services are at least 20 points higher than those of the institutions in the bottom quartile. Table 3.7 also reveals that institutions in the top quartile for transition rate had substantially smaller percentages of students receiving financial aid or loan aid than those in the bottom quartile.

TABLE 3.5

Enrollment and Student Demographics at Postsecondary Institutions in Top Quartile and Bottom Quartile by Transition Rate

	Top Quartile (N = 117)	*Bottom Quartile (N = 119)*
Total enrollment (mean)	6,981	8,662
Younger than 20 (median %)	29.4	27.3
20–24 years old (median %)	28.5	32.8
25–29 years old (median %)	12.1	12.2
30 years and older (median %)	29.7	25.4
Women (median %)	60.0	60.0
White, non-Hispanic (median %)	76.0	69.0
Black, non-Hispanic (median %)	5.0	7.0
Hispanic (median %)	3.0	3.0
Asian/Pacific Islander (median %)	1.0	1.0

Note. Median percentages of institutions in each quartile were reported for age and ethnicity distribution; thus, percentages do not add up to 100%.

TABLE 3.6

Admission, Retention, and Graduation Rates at Postsecondary Institutions in Top Quartile and Bottom Quartile by Transition Rate

	Top Quartile (%) (N = 117)	*Bottom Quartile (%) (N = 119)*
Open enrollment policy	97.4	67.2
Full-time retention rate (median)[a]	57.0	59.0
Part-time retention rate (median)[b]	39.0	40.0
Graduation rate (median)[c]	25.0	28.0

[a]The rate is the percentage of the fall full-time cohort from the prior year that reenrolled at the institution as either full- or part-time in the current year.
[b]The rate is the percentage of the fall part-time cohort from the prior year that reenrolled at the institution as either full- or part-time in the current year.
[c]The rate of first-time, full-time degree or certificate-seeking students is calculated as the total number of completers within 150% of normal time divided by the cohort.

TABLE 3.7

Selected Student Services and Support Provided at Postsecondary Institutions in Top Quartile and Bottom Quartile by Transition Rate

	Top Quartile (N = 117)	Bottom Quartile (N = 119)
Remedial services (%)	100.0	89.1
Employment services for students (%)	98.3	91.6
Placement services for completers (%)	91.5	91.6
On-campus day care for students' children (%)	75.2	52.1
Occupational education (%)	100.0	74.0
Adult basic remedial or high school equivalent (%)	100.0	69.8
Distance-learning opportunities (%)	100.0	89.9
Weekend/evening college (%)	41.0	37.0
Students receiving any financial aid (median %)	63.0	81.0
Students receiving student loan aid (median %)	12.0	21.0

Discussion

Reaching economic stability is critical for adult learners and requires education beyond a GED credential. Results from this research have shown that postsecondary institutions are a major channel for adults without a high school credential to earn a GED credential, and in many instances they retain those who have passed the GED test for PSE. What can be done at institutions enrolling students with GED credentials, particularly at public two-year colleges, to enhance enrollment, persistence, and graduation rates is a very important and urgent education policy issue (OVAE, 2010).

At first glance, whether a GED passer tests on or off campus may seem to make little difference. However, differences by degree type are striking and may indicate varying experiences depending on the level of institution and postsecondary program selected. GED testing centers based in postsecondary institutions, primarily community colleges, eventually transitioned more GED passers to programs offering postsecondary certificates, at least initially, than to associate's degree programs, whereas the opposite tended to occur for GED passers testing off campus. One explanation might be that the community college GED testing center (or an on-campus adult education program) may offer transitional services to encourage enrollment into certificate programs. Or potential students who are interested in short-term college programs found that they need a GED credential as a prerequisite and are then referred to the GED testing center (or an adult education program) housed on campus. In contrast, GED passers testing off campus may tend to think of traditional associate's degrees rather than a short-term postsecondary diploma or certificate when they consider postsecondary programs in community colleges. Do off-campus GED testing centers, such as school-based or community-based adult education centers or correctional facilities, refer GED passers to associate's degree programs more readily? While these potential explanations are speculative given the data available, differences by degree type deserve further qualitative consideration.

For GED passers who test and enroll on campus, it is intriguing that they enroll and ultimately graduate sooner than those who later enroll in a different institution, as shown in Figure 3.1. On average, those enrolling at a different institution tended to enroll 10 months later. Even though they took less time to complete a certificate or associate's degree, postsecondary enrollees at a different institution tended to remain an additional five months behind. During these five months, their counterparts could potentially be earning a higher wage, if offered as a result of the certificate or degree (OVAE, 2010; SREB, 2010; Tyler & Lofstrum, 2010), or start pursuing a

Figure 3.1 Average number of months from passing GED test to PSE enrollment, and to PSE certificate or associate's degree by enrollee location.

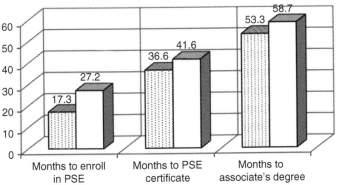

higher degree. This finding suggests that, building on the learning momentum of the GED graduates and their increasing familiarity with the PSE environment, it is urgent for PSE institutions that have on-campus GED testing centers to engage in proactive recruiting of GED graduates and to invest in transition programs.

The lower transition rates at four-year (or above) public institutions present a concern and lead to further questions. Even though traditionally the majority of GED graduates have enrolled at community colleges, the level of institutional readiness to accept and retain GED passers in PSE as a subpopulation of nontraditional adult learners is an issue of growing importance for four-year institutions because transitioning and graduating nontraditional adult learners is now becoming a key component of U.S. higher education. Do differences in transition rates relate to disparities in specific services, such as on-campus day care, occupational education, or adult education programs? If community colleges that consistently offer these services thereby increase their appeal to GED passers, more research on the role of institutional services could assist postsecondary institutions, particularly those with outreach to nontraditional students in general, in evaluating PSE barrier reduction (OVAE, 2010) and program outcomes such as retention and graduation.

A final point worth reflection is the list of top 100 institutions in terms of PSE transition rate. Both environmental and institutional factors can contribute to the variances in transition rate. For example, in a rural area or a remote small city, perhaps only one postsecondary institution is located within close commuting distance. It is therefore highly likely that GED graduates tested there would enroll at the same institution for certificate or degree programs because there are no convenient alternatives nearby. In small cities where PSE options may be more plentiful, other explanations could include local employer needs (SREB, 2010) or the growing presence of integrated adult education and technical programs (OVAE, 2010). Employers in small cities with a limited pool of educated workers may need to rely on local community colleges to recruit and prepare adults with low skills to pass the GED test and complete technical courses of study as quickly and efficiently as possible.

However, for postsecondary educators and policymakers, a more imperative charge from the top-100 list is to investigate what institutional programs or public policies could have prompted a higher proportion of GED graduates into timely PSE enrollment. Researchers could examine qualitatively what specific transition efforts lead to reduced time to enrollment and to graduation and how those efforts are planned and implemented. Case studies on some of these high performers will help to shed light on future PSE transition programs.

References

American Council on Education (ACE). (2003–2010). *2002–2009 GED testing program statistical reports.* Washington, DC: Author.

American Council on Education (ACE). (2011). *2010 GED testing program statistical report.* Washington, DC: Author.

Bound, J., Lovenheim, M., & Turner, S. (2010). *Increasing time to baccalaureate degree in the United States.* NBER Working Paper 15892. Cambridge, MA: National Bureau of Economic Research.

Cohen, J. (1988). *Statistical power analysis for the behavioral sciences* (2nd ed.). Hillsdale, NJ: Lawrence Erlbaum Associates.

Council for Advancement of Adult Literacy (CAAL). (2008). *Reach higher, America: Overcoming crisis in the U.S. workforce.* New York, NY: Author.

GED Testing Service. (2011). *Testing center profile 2010.* Unpublished survey report.

Guison-Dowdy, A., & Patterson, M. B. (2011a). *Journeys through college: Postsecondary transitions and outcomes of GED® test passers.* Washington, DC: American Council on Education. Retrieved from www.gedtestingservice.com

Office of Vocational and Adult Education (OVAE). (2010). *Postsecondary education transition: A summary of the findings from two literature reviews.* Washington, DC: U.S. Department of Education.

Patterson, M. B., Zhang, J., Song, W., & Guison-Dowdy, A. (2010). *Crossing the bridge: GED credentials and postsecondary outcomes (Year 1 report).* Washington, DC: American Council on Education. Available at www.gedtestingservice.com

Reder, S. (2007). *Adult education and postsecondary success.* New York, NY: Council for Advancement of Adult Literacy. Retrieved from www.nationalcommissionon adultliteracy.org/content/rederpolicybriefrev10807.pdf

Reder, S. (2010). *Adult literacy development and economic growth.* Washington, DC: National Institute for Literacy.

Southern Regional Education Board (SREB). (2010). *A smart move in tough times: How SREB states can strengthen adult learning and the work force.* Retrieved from http://publications.sreb.org/2010/10E06_Smart_Move.pdf

Tyler, J., & Lofstrum, M. (2010). Is the GED an effective route to postsecondary education for school dropouts? *Economics of Education Review, 29*(2010), 813–825.

Zhang, J., Guison-Dowdy, A., Patterson, M. B., & Song, W. (2011). *Crossing the bridge: GED credentials and postsecondary educational outcomes: Year two report.* Washington, DC: American Council on Education.

PART TWO

THE VOICE OF THE STATEWIDE LEADER AND ADMINISTRATOR

4

REDEFINING COMMUNITY COLLEGE STUDENT SUCCESS

Helton "Hep" M. Aldridge

> *The whole purpose of education is to turn mirrors into windows.*
>
> —Sydney J. Harris

I n this chapter I investigate the definition of student success at the community college level as it relates to more nontraditional students in the postsecondary education system, such as those who enter with a General Education Development (GED®) certificate. In doing so, I briefly review historical information on the topic, explore the learning-centered philosophies put forth by Terry O'Banion, and examine the work done by Vincent Tinto. This will help in the development of an overall picture of how a student's success can be more effectively facilitated and more accurately defined.

While Tinto examined the persistence and success of the university student, O'Banion focused on the community college. Interestingly, both researchers share much common ground in their theories. They have both identified interactions between students and faculty, strong academic programs, and extracurricular activities as a strong foundation for student persistence and success. Both Tinto and O'Banion assert that creating a sense of affiliation with, or belonging to, an institution has a positive effect on student outcomes. It should be noted that for freshmen living on campus in the university setting, the opportunities for these types of activities may be more easily accessible than for those enrolled at a nonresidential institution.

However, O'Banion posits that community colleges can and should require more effort and resource allocation within their unique learning environments in order to create the same feelings of affiliation. O'Banion believes that all individuals at the community college must work together to create this environment, and that each department plays a specific role. In this approach, student affairs and the educational environment are viewed in a new light. Much of the historical research done in this area has put the primary emphasis on the academic side of the house. Through O'Banion's efforts, student affairs is now being recognized as a key partner in helping students achieve their educational goals.

Student Affiliation

Traditionally, institutions of higher education have been strongly committed to academic integration as a vehicle for student success; however, the overarching educational environment itself has often not been recognized as an integral component for student retention and success. This has been a major oversight because the literature tells us that "environmental support compensates for weak academic support but academic support will not compensate for weak environmental support" (Bean & Metzner, 1985, p. 492). Student affiliation with the institution therefore becomes a major component of student retention, and it takes on major significance for community college students and institutions. Although community colleges typically serve a commuter student population, there appears to be no reason why these students cannot develop a sense of affiliation with the institution, especially if the institution works to foster a sense of community among students and creates a positive learning environment that transcends the classroom.

A Learner-Centered Approach

While the classroom mission is taking precedent in many community colleges, through the learning-centered method, it is widely acknowledged that all areas within an institution play a vital role in the ultimate success of the student and the institution. For community colleges that want to become more learning-centered, it will make a difference in policies, programs, and practices if learning is embedded in the institutional culture as the highest priority. Once again, O'Banion (1999) offers a road map for institutions that are implementing learning-centered strategies:

> Community colleges that wish to make this perspective an integral part of their culture can ask two basic questions that will help keep faculty, staff, trustees, and administrators focused on the major goal; one, does this

action improve and expand learning and two, how do we know this action improves and expands learning? These two questions can be applied to any area of activity in an institution to help its members become more aware of the importance of learning in everyday practice.

The current literature on learning-centered methodologies shows the importance of a broad-based approach to providing students with a wide variety of learning opportunities. This would include activities both inside and outside the traditional classroom. In that light, at community colleges across the nation, enrollment management has recently come to the forefront in the areas of student affairs and student development as the dominant methodology for dealing with student retention, recruitment, marketing, and related student services with the ultimate goal of college completion. Under this broad umbrella of enrollment management, student affairs administrators find themselves taking a fresh look at the role and responsibility of their departments. This review has allowed the inclusion of the learning-centered approach to education as a driving force within the operational structure of student affairs departments and divisions. To this end, enrollment management and the revitalizing opportunities it brings with it offer student affairs administrators a fresh palette with which to paint the new image of student affairs and student success for the 21st century.

Student Affairs and Academic Affairs in Partnership

While faculty oversee classroom activities, the student affairs administrator is responsible for a host of critical campus operations such as admissions, registration, records, advising, counseling, assessment, testing, placement, services for students with disabilities, and, in some institutions, financial aid. While these areas have historically provided services to students, in light of a more holistic approach, it becomes necessary to go far beyond this limiting view of their function. In terms of student success and learning-centeredness, the important factors are not only what services student affairs provides, but *how* they provide the services and *the context or environment in which they are provided.* The changes in postsecondary education over recent years have dramatically altered the theater in which community colleges operate. Proprietary schools, corporate trade industry schools, and private sector training have increasingly moved the community college out of the "only game in town" position for the place-bound learner and made it a competing entity within this evolving educational context. It is increasingly evident that the way in which community colleges do business, and the types of services they offer their students, must be as progressive and dynamic as the environment in which they now find themselves. A variety of new concerns thus become part of the student affairs professional's world. As stated in *Educating by*

Design, "The idea of campus environment, culture, and civility in the delivery of services and dealings with students must now become key elements in the planning and implementation of programs and services" (Strange & Banning, 2001).

Starting from the assumption that student success is the goal of the community college, and that it is the responsibility of the faculty and staff to facilitate this success, it then becomes important to understand the relationship between the academic side of the house and the student affairs side of the house. In the past, a rift between these two institutional divisions has often existed with each entity blaming the other for a variety of operational ills. The learning-centered approach requires that this rift, if it still exists, be bridged so that both sides work together to accomplish the goal of student success. To do so, it is imperative that student affairs be viewed as a full and equal partner in this endeavor. According to O'Banion (1999), "The new science of management and leadership prescribes flattened organizations, open communication and empowered participation, [which] makes a strong case for involving all stakeholders in major reform efforts" (p. 23). The link between the learning-centered philosophy and its benefits to retention and student persistence are obvious. The learning-centered approach focuses on students becoming successful learners and achieving their educational goals. This, of course, cannot happen if the student chooses not to persist. Therefore, an understanding and melding of learning-centered theory and retention is beneficial if significant learning-centered change within student affairs is to be achieved. Additionally, the partnership between academic and student affairs becomes a critical component of this change. The work of Vincent Tinto provides a graphic representation that begins to give us a sense of this partnership. Tinto's model for student departure, or the longitudinal process model of dropout decision making, has as two of its major components academic integration and social integration.

Social Integration

The literature shows us that the majority of the students who drop out of community colleges do so for reasons other than academic problems; therefore, the idea of social integration becomes one of major importance when looking at student success. It is a key factor that has been largely overlooked until recently in the community college setting. Another major component of Tinto's model is the student's commitment to the institution. This commitment translates into the student's desire to become affiliated with a particular institution of higher education.

This very well may be a driving factor for most university students, but I would suggest that in the community college, although commitment is still a key factor, there is a reversal in how this phenomenon functions in the equation of student persistence. For community colleges, which typically lack the glamour appeal of residential universities, it is reasonable to suggest that the commitment of the institution to the student, rather than vice versa, is the major factor in whether or not the student persists and succeeds in reaching his or her educational goals. This commitment can be expressed in a number of ways. The quality of teaching faculty at the institution; the variety and breadth of curriculum; the resources available to students both academic and social; the appearance of the campus, buildings, classrooms, and offices; the ease of access for all students to these resources; and the attitude of all support staff are all important components of this theory. In fact, institutional commitment to the student within the community college setting may be the critical factor in determining whether a student chooses to persist or drop out. In researching this idea, I have identified four major areas for departmental assessment within the learning-centered context: Atmosphere, attitude, access, and policies and procedures. They are critical components that provide a holistic framework within which to evaluate the learning-centeredness and student success orientation of an institution.

Atmosphere is the student's first impression of the campus grounds and the buildings' exterior and interior, lighting, colors, and signage. These all create a feeling before the student even speaks to anyone. Also important is whether an institution creates spaces for students to socially interact with one another, and with faculty and staff outside of traditional classrooms and professional settings.

Attitude describes the attitude of personnel on campus. This includes everyone from grounds crew, security, and admissions staff, to advisors and support staff. These are likely the first people whom students encounter when they arrive on campus, long before any interaction with the faculty. Are these staff members welcoming, energetic, helpful, and actually happy doing their jobs?

Access reflects whether students and employees have access to the information and tools they need to do their jobs effectively. These resources can run the gamut from updated printed and electronic materials for students and staff regarding curriculum changes, faculty contact info, and administrative procedures within their departments, as well as up-to-date computer systems for both students and employees. This could also include registration, admissions, advising hours of operations, library access and hours, learning labs and tutoring hours, and faculty availability.

Finally, do the *policies and procedures* of the department or institution enhance or impede student progress? Is the institution itself building super-highways for students and staff to navigate, or are they throwing up roadblocks due to ill-defined or outdated policies and procedures?

All of these factors are essential for student success and should be used to provide feedback for continual improvement in all departments of the institution.

With the aforementioned aspects, a new model for student success in the community college emerges.

A New Model for Community College Student Success

Using Tinto's longitudinal process model as a starting point, the AB paradigm, or the community college student success model (Figure 4.1), more appropriately describes the longitudinal progression of students through the community college educational process, ultimately resulting in the student's success or goal achievement.

In this model, success includes degree attainment but goes on to encompass the variety of options available to the community college student. It takes into consideration the full partnership of academic and student affairs, as well as the commitment of the institution to the student, a component vital to student success. Student affairs now becomes an integral part of this institutional commitment to the student, improving retention and, ultimately, student success. It is noted that a comprehensive student affairs program mandates the delivery of a strongly integrated and dynamic array of services that are aligned with the academic and administrative areas of the college. A program of this nature is intended to develop institutional and personal behaviors, which results in a culture that is fully student centered and committed to the success of each student. According to Ender, Chand, and Thornton (1996), "Programs with these characteristics integrate the talents, resources and energies of the academic and student affairs communities

Figure 4.1 Community college student success model.

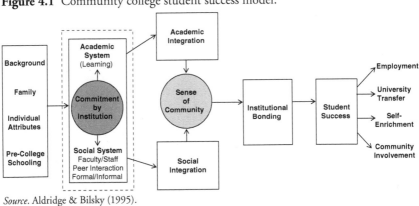

Source. Aldridge & Bilsky (1995).

to provide a relevant and holistic college experience for students." Through this learning-centered approach, the student develops a true identification of self with the institution and is cognizant of an ongoing symbiotic relationship (Bilsky, 2000). The student comes to understand that there are benefits to becoming enmeshed with the institution. The institution, in turn, rewards this "loyalty" both tangibly and intangibly. For their efforts, students can become more visible within the administrative/instructional framework of the college; they often develop into student leaders whose input becomes respected and well received. The institution benefits from this direct student feedback, which allows needs to be identified and addressed before they become actual concerns or problems.

With the open-door policies of the community college, students are often nontraditional, adult learners who come to college from a variety of backgrounds and with varying degrees of college readiness. Community college students may include recent high school graduates, working adults, returning students, GED completers, and single parents. Many of these students fall into the "at-risk" category and require institutional assistance and support prior to, and during, their enrollment in order to enhance their chances of success.

The AB Paradigm

The AB paradigm embraces the holistic nature of institution/student interactions and provides a frame of reference for community college practitioners to evaluate their own institutional setting. It also becomes a valuable tool for the transformation of student affairs within the context of learning-centeredness.

The germane portion of the AB model is the institutional commitment cell (Figure 4.2). This reflects a commitment by the institution to create an environment supportive of learning in its fullest sense. This is a departure from many current theoretical models in which the definition of *institutional commitment* is the student's commitment to the institution (how strong the desire within the student is to enroll at a particular institution). Tinto, Astin, and others have frequently used this line of thinking with the university model, in which the student's original goal is degree completion and motivation to affiliate with a selected institution is strong.

According to the AB paradigm, if institutional commitment is strong in fully supporting the academic and social integration of the student, then a sense of community can form. This will lead to the student understanding that the institution does care about his or her success. Ultimately (and optimally), a bonding then occurs between the student and the institution within

Figure 4.2 AB paradigm model.

Academic System
Faculty-Led Curriculum

**Commitment
By
Institution**

Social System
Faculty/Staff
Peer Interactions
Formal/Informal

the context of a climate in which the student develops a positive relationship with the college. This "climate of caring" by nature and design nurtures and supports student persistence and, ultimately, student success.

Conclusion

For years many institutions have defined *success* as degree completion. States would have us use the same measure for community college students. Although states need some measure of accountability for community colleges, and institutions need to facilitate degree completion, it is ill conceived to use such a limiting measure as degree completion for the community college student. After all, who ultimately decides if the student is successful? I would suggest that the students themselves make this decision. Thus, the full range of academic possibilities available at the community college can be taken into consideration, and success can be measured in a variety of ways. Certainly degree or certificate completion is important, but what about the individual who is currently employed in the computer industry and needs to take one or two new programming language courses to improve the opportunity for advancement or promotion? What about an individual working in the welding industry who needs one semester of training to learn a new welding technique in order to qualify for a higher-paying position? Although neither of these individuals would be considered *completers* by state definition after taking these courses, in both instances, the students will have met "their" educational goals and felt successful in their educational endeavors.

One can argue that community colleges offer a flexible variety of degree and nondegree educational options for their students and that many working students take advantage of this opportunity. So when evaluating a college's performance should there not be a broader definition considered for *student success* that takes into account this institutional flexibility and expands the definition of *student success* as suggested in the AB paradigm? Perhaps it is time for policymakers to broaden the definition of *performance* in performance-based funding. For example, it may be worthwhile to consider the following additional options when defining a student's performance, such as counting transfers in the formula; holding funding in escrow or pro-rating for students who stop-out or only make small progress each semester; counting students with GEDs earned; counting English for Academic Purposes (EAP) courses and developmental education courses completed; and exempting any students in non-degree seeking status who are looking to take courses for personal or professional development (or perhaps devise a way to reward that as well).

Institutions may also need to think about creating tangible completion points that can be more easily counted and tracked by policymakers. Can there be a certificate or an award for students who complete remediation, who earn credits for professional development, who complete EAP programs, or who earn industry certifications? Perhaps it is time to redefine community college outcomes more specifically and demonstrate to policymakers the full value of the community college mission. As more states move to performance-based funding, it is imperative for community college leaders to work with policymakers to craft comprehensive legislation that recognizes and rewards the full spectrum of community college success and completion.

As the demographic, economic, technological, and social needs of our country change, our "internal" traditional concepts of how to best meet the postsecondary educational needs of our students require revitalization. Clearly, the burden and responsibility for student success rests not solely on how policymakers measure success, but also on how community college educators reevaluate and reconfigure what has become a dated approach to meeting the needs of college students with vastly different educational, environmental, financial, and personal needs than those in the past. Just as our students are required to commit to their education and career, our colleges need to fully commit to providing holistic educational environments. A focus on learning-centered atmospheres, attitudes, access to information and services, and student-centered policies and procedures will foster student success and allow community colleges to realize the full potential of their mission.

References

Aldridge, H., & Bilsky, J. (1995). *AB paradigm: A community college student success model.* Ann Arbor, Michigan. UMI Dissertation Services.

Bean, J. P., & Metzner, B. S. (1985). *A conceptual model of nontraditional undergraduate student attrition. Review of Educational Research, 55,* 485–540.

Bilsky, J. H. (2000). *Student satisfaction among select demographic groups at a Florida community college.* (Unpublished doctoral dissertation). College of Education, University of Florida, Gainesville.

Ender, K., Chand, S., & Thornton, J. (1996). Student affairs in the community college: Promoting student success and learning. In S. C. Ender, F. B. Newton, & R. B. Caple (Eds.), *Contributing to learning: The role of student affairs. New Directions for Student Services, 75.* San Francisco, CA: Jossey-Bass.

O'Banion, T. (1999). *Launching a learning centered college.* (Monograph). Mission Viejo, CA: League for Innovation in the Community College.

Strange, C., & Banning, J. (2001). *Educating by design: Creating campus learning environments that work.* San Francisco, CA: Jossey-Bass.

5

STATE OF EDUCATIONAL TRENDS

The Developmental Education Dilemma

Mark A. Heinrich

The difference between a successful person and others is not a lack of strength, not a lack of knowledge, but rather a lack of will.

—Vince Lombardi

The initial or foundational credential for most educated persons in the United States is the high school diploma or its equivalency. Without a high school diploma, an individual's lifetime earnings potential is significantly hindered, as are countless other opportunities. One of the largest groups of underprepared but skilled individuals in the United States are those working-age adults who, for a variety of reasons, lack the high school credential. Many individuals without a high school diploma or its equivalency are often described as extremely apprehensive and even terrified about the prospect of returning to school or participating in adult education courses. Embarrassment, humiliation, or appearing foolish in front of their peers or others much younger often drives the irrational fears that invade this group's psyche. Interestingly, although this group often suffers from unfounded fears, they are typically very capable individuals who have had "life happen" to them, making it difficult or impossible for them to complete their education on the traditional timeline.

As those who regularly work with individuals lacking their high school credentials understand, these individuals are often very capable, mature, and excited about gaining the needed qualifications essential to be productive workers, family members, and citizens. When given the confidence, appropriate and necessary academic support, skilled and professional tutoring, and genuine encouragement, they almost always succeed at a very high level. Furthermore, this population will make up much of our nation's future skilled workforce.

In Alabama, it is estimated that in excess of 600,000 working-age adults have no high school credentials. This statistic is staggering but fairly typical of many states and should not be tolerated. With many "boomers" on the verge of retirement, states are scrambling to train and educate the next generation of skilled workers within the United States. In our nation's quest to provide a labor force for the 21st century, it has become increasingly clear that the traditional pipeline (17- to 23-year-olds) simply is not plentiful enough to adequately fill the growing workforce needs. As a result, the nontraditional student populations should and will play a more robust role in meeting the increased workforce demands. High-touch educational programming; well-crafted adult education classes; and highly skilled, professionally prepared tutors and advisors are essential ingredients in promoting success for those seeking the all-important high school credential or General Education Development (GED®) certificate.

In this chapter I make some very bold recommendations regarding the preparation and support of high-risk nontraditional and underprepared students. These suggestions are labor intensive and can be costly. However, the cost of an underprepared workforce is far greater than any amount a state should and must invest to properly prepare its citizens for the future. It is my belief that our nation has a moral and ethical obligation to effectively meet the escalating needs of those lacking high school credentials, as well as those who are underprepared, regardless of cost. The recommendations in this chapter specifically address how best to prepare and support two very ·important groups of students: those preparing for the GED, and those who fall into the growing category of being underprepared for postsecondary education despite having earned a GED credential or its equivalent.

Our Story

When I began my tenure as president of Shelton State Community College in Tuscaloosa, Alabama, in January 2008, serious concerns were beginning to emerge regarding the large population of underprepared students on our campuses. Almost immediately after my arrival at Shelton State, it became painfully evident to me that our developmental education program was failing to achieve satisfactory results and needed a restructuring centered around fresh approaches and proven ideas. At that time, the existing program's results were nothing less than dismal, with many of these underprepared students mired in developmental education limbo, despite the best efforts of dedicated practitioners.

This problem, of course, is not limited to Shelton State, or even to community colleges in Alabama. It is no secret that a large percentage of first-time students entering the nation's community colleges are not prepared academically for the classroom challenges they are about to face, often landing them in developmental education courses intended to raise their proficiency in reading, writing, or math to college-ready levels, but often leaving them with little more than a deep sense of failure. Two different analyses indicate that nearly 60% of community college students take at least one developmental education course during their academic career, although that number likely undercounts the number of underprepared students arriving on community college campuses because some of them are exempted or find ways to skirt the classes (Bailey, 2009).

A distressing percentage of the students who end up in community college developmental education programs never progress past the pre-college courses meant to bring them up to speed. According to the Community College Research Center (Bailey, 2009), roughly 45% of community college students who place into a developmental math course just one level below the college level never successfully complete remediation requirements. The odds are considerably lower for those students who begin three or more levels below college-level math, with a mere 17% completing the entire developmental sequence, the Community College Research Center reports. Specifically, when analyzing the vast number of students who possess GED certificates and who are enrolled in developmental education courses, this serves as a major deterrent to postsecondary education success. As the chancellor of the Alabama Community College System since September 2012, I find that this issue frequently commands my attention today. Like many administrators and educators across the nation, I fully realize developmental education has become an extremely contentious issue; I also know it is a problem requiring action. The key question is, Just what needs to be done?

Putting a New System in Place

Similar to the developmental education programs at many community colleges, Shelton State's clearly needed a redesign when my tenure began. Over a two-year period beginning in 2009, a group of faculty and staff members at Shelton State overhauled the community college's entire developmental education program, creating a comprehensive approach that features ongoing innovations in instructional methods; a meticulous, even intrusive advising component that seeks to engage the student; and flexible and effective tutoring that meets the needs of today's underprepared students. Think of it as the "pit bull approach," grabbing onto the student and not letting go. The truth is you cannot just place a developmental education student in front of a computer and expect a successful outcome; many institutions, however, merely go through the motions when it comes to programs for underprepared students.

Based on the early outcomes at Shelton State, community colleges nationwide would benefit from this kind of philosophical change in the manner in which they deliver support services to high-risk, underprepared students. Yes, the up-front costs of providing an expanded developmental education program are daunting and substantial, but the cost associated with non-completers is far higher. As Charles Claxton points out, *"Bad remediation costs about as much as good remediation"* (Boylan & Saxon, 2005, p. 9; emphasis added). With so much on the line, it is critically important that policymakers, community college administrators, and developmental education professionals continue to seek sound approaches and proper solutions to this very real problem.

I believe it is time for state policymakers to look realistically at their developmental education programs and guidelines and bring them in line with the literature. As educators and administrators with precious few available dollars, we may be persuaded into believing that there is a simple fix to the underprepared student epidemic in an attempt to save dollars and ignore the research that spells out the most effective strategies. It is very true that quality developmental education is neither sexy nor cost-effective. Few, if any, educators will achieve fame or tenure by helping a student reach competency in remedial arithmetic.

Quality, data-driven developmental education programs can and do make a big difference if they are properly designed and correctly managed, which is why Shelton State invested significant time and money in this noble cause. The lessons we have learned at Shelton State may be of assistance to many administrators and educators striving to better serve underprepared students in the 21st century. At the very least, this ambitious effort can become a part of the conversation regarding the future of developmental education in America.

At Shelton State, where the average fall enrollment is about 5,200 students, between 55% and 74% of incoming freshmen in the years 2007 through 2009 needed at least one developmental education course. While those numbers seem high, an even more distressing finding was this: Successful academic outcomes for students placing in developmental education classes were simply too rare. Between 2007 and 2009, pass rates in all developmental education courses for Shelton State students in the fall semester averaged 42%, while the three-year average for students in the spring semester between 2008 and 2010 was even lower: just 39%. Pass rates for some individual classes were even more woeful. In the foundational mathematics course called MTH 098, the average pass rate for Shelton State's fall semester students between 2007 and 2009 was 25%; it did not improve significantly for spring semester students between 2008 and 2010, with a passing rate of just 26%. Obviously, dismaying results of this kind have deeply negative implications for retention efforts—and again Shelton State is not alone in this regard.

Developmental math, as those MTH 098 results suggest, represents a significant barrier to attainment for many community college students around the nation. As research by Dr. Hunter Boylan and others points out, one in three first-time community college students ends up in developmental math—and a third fail the course the first time. Boylan, the director of the National Center for Developmental Education and a professor of higher education at North Carolina's Appalachian State University, notes that many students have to retake developmental math two or three times before they pass it. Some students never pass, become frustrated and filled with a sense of hopelessness, and quietly drop out of college. Foundational math, though, is essential to attainment, because it is a gateway course needed for academic transfer as well as vocational training programs. This underscores how failure in developmental math can severely limit career opportunities for many students and can have the effect of literally shutting them out of a lifetime of learning. "It should be obvious that we must find ways to do a better job in developmental mathematics," Boylan writes. "We cannot continue to simply fail large numbers of students in developmental mathematics and then ask them to retake the same course as their only alternative" (as cited in Kelley & Murphy, 2006, p. ii).

Around the time I began the presidency at Shelton State, there was a renewed emphasis in the nation's higher education circles on completion, and colleges around the United States were beginning to recognize and address the abysmal success rates of their developmental education courses. In prior years, with so many students pursuing a community college education, few administrators were paying much attention to the large number of underprepared students who became part of the revolving door of failure that unfortunately is typical of community college education. But times and attitudes were changing as the completion agenda began to quickly move to the forefront in higher education. In addition, there has been a growing appreciation of the community college system's role in preparing America's workforce for the in-demand jobs of the 21st century, jobs that demand postsecondary education or skills training. To state it another way, it has become clear that community colleges need to step up their educational game in an effort to satisfy important local workforce development needs at a time of economic crisis, as expectations are quickly rising in this regard.

A Matter of Ethics

There are moral and ethical issues that community college educators need to consider as they devise plans to address dreadful developmental education pass rates and assist this large population of underprepared students in living up to their full potential as workers and citizens. The bottom line for us as an institution is that we were letting students down with poorly designed and executed developmental education programs. Around the country at this particular time, many were acknowledging that an overhaul of developmental education was long overdue if acceptable and necessary results were to be achieved. It quickly became clear that the time was right for changes at Shelton State.

Despite decades of research, however, it has to be noted that there is no recognized one-size-fits-all approach that outlines precisely how to restructure developmental education programs to ensure improvement in student achievement. The reality is that the entire developmental education system "is characterized by uncertainty, a lack of consensus on either the definition of being college ready or the best strategies to pursue high costs, and varied and often unknown benefits" (Bailey, 2009, p. 2). Disagreement over which developmental education approaches are the most effective is probably as high today as it has ever been. Recently, questions have even arisen over whether developmental education, as we have known it, should be eliminated altogether and replaced by an approach that places underprepared students in mainstream classes and provides them with extra supports to help them succeed. Complete College America, Inc. has been leading the charge in the campaign, flatly stating that developmental education just does not work as it has been structured. In a joint statement titled *Core Principles for Transforming Remedial Education,* it was said,

> The research is clear: Remedial education as it is commonly designed and delivered is not the aid to student success that we all hoped. It is time for policymakers and institutional leaders to take their cue from new research and emerging evidence-based practices that are leading the way toward a fundamentally new model of instruction and support for students who enter college not optimally prepared for college-level work. (Charles A. Dana Center, Complete College America, Inc., Education Commission of the States, & Jobs for the Future, 2012)

Many researchers have countered that this contention is extreme and that, although flawed, developmental education still has its place in helping underprepared students overcome academic deficits. As Boylan and Saxon (2005) have noted, developmental education is often very poorly administered, a major factor leading to disappointing results. "Providing effective remediation is not a mysterious proposition," they write in *What Works in Remediation: Lessons from 30 Years of Research.* "We know how to do it. We simply do not use what we know" (p. 9).

A Statewide Approach

In recent years, some state community college systems have decided to stop leaving the structure of developmental education programs up to individual schools. A few states have implemented systemwide initiatives that sprang from unflinching inspections of their programs, identifying the shortcomings that had to be addressed. Massachusetts, for instance, took a hard look at its developmental education programs in the late 1980s and made a series of constructive recommendations regarding the best teaching and administrative practices (Sperling, 2009). Later, the "100% Math Initiative" was launched to improve the quality of developmental mathematics instruction at Massachusetts community colleges. The report issued in 2006 that stemmed from this effort, *Building a Foundation for Student Success in Developmental Mathematics*, also noted that the developmental math sequence is a tremendous barrier for underprepared students while highlighting the urgent need to increase success rates in those classes (Massachusetts Community College Executive Office, 2006). The audit states,

> In particular, the "100% Math Initiative" focused on developing an improved set of approaches, structures, and systems driven by specific student and faculty needs that would foster and support the types of critical interactions between faculty and students that are the bedrock of success among developmental mathematics students. (p. iv)

The initiative produced many sound ideas. One of its recommendations was that developmental math instructors at Massachusetts community colleges begin by teaching students basic study skills, including note and test taking and effective self-studying. It also stressed the critical role of training and professional development for developmental education instructors. The initiative recommended that the state's community colleges create the position of campus mathematics coordinator and establish math centers where students could receive tutoring, reference materials, and supplemental instruction. Additionally, the report recommended the creation of a statewide Developmental Mathematics Leadership Group to coordinate the implementation of the initiative's recommendations.

Virginia is another state that has launched a major overhaul of its community college developmental education program. In 2004, the Virginia Community College System joined Achieving the Dream, the national nongovernmental reform network that aims at increasing student success in higher education, and examined its developmental education outcomes, which it found to be unsatisfactory. By 2009, when the Virginia system joined the Developmental Education Initiative, the planning process for the redesign of its developmental education effort was in full force. The goals laid down in its Achieve 2015 overhaul were ambitious: a 50% increase in the number of Virginia community college students who complete a degree, transfer to a four-year school, or earn a workforce credential; and a 75% increase for those students typically underrepresented in higher education. (In 2013, both of these goals were restated to triple the increase.) As a result of this effort, the structure of developmental education in Virginia's community colleges was dramatically changed. Developmental math is being taught as modules, with students taking only the modules they need based on the results of the placement test and the individual student's academic requirements. Developmental English, which integrates reading and writing courses, is being taught in tiers, with three direct pathways to college-level English, ensuring that developmental education requirements can be met in one year. Virginia took the effort a step further. Its redesign embraced the idea that the system's improvement goals would fail unless the community college students who start in developmental education succeed. The following goals were established: (a) decrease the number of students needing developmental education in the first place, (b) reduce the time spent in developmental education courses, and (c) boost college completion rates of those students starting off in developmental education. The results of this very ambitious approach are being closely monitored.

Texas, where 41% of all students enrolled in higher education required some form of developmental education, has been particularly aggressive on the reform front (Texas Higher Education Coordinating Board, 2012). Back in 2006, the Texas Higher Education Coordinating Board established what it calls "summer bridge programs," aimed at decreasing the need for developmental education and improving student success. The program is now offered to high school juniors and seniors, as well as to recent high school graduates who fell below the college-ready standard on assessment tests. The coordinating board reports that its research demonstrates that the intensive summer bridge programs have decreased the need for developmental education, prompting the organization to begin developing a model program based on best practices that can be scaled statewide after a trial period.

In 2009, the Higher Education Policy Institute of the Texas Higher Education Coordinating Board made a series of sweeping recommendations aimed at improving developmental education outcomes in that state. The recommendations began with a call for a mandatory assessment of incoming students using a statewide system that can pinpoint a student's academic needs and track his or her progress over time. The Texas formula called for systematic placement into appropriate developmental education programs after that assessment, with appropriate supports and interventions for individual students determined through a data-driven decision-making process. Other recommendations called for the implementation of enhanced academic advising, the establishment of small learning communities, and the identification of effective curricular standards and developmental education teaching methods. The organization underscored that developmental education courses should be taught by high-quality instructors who have access to professional development opportunities. A final recommendation called for colleges to reach out to K–12 schools in an attempt to better align systems and curriculum, reducing the need for developmental education classes for more college-bound students.

In 2010, the Texas Higher Education Coordinating Board launched developmental education demonstration pilot projects at five community colleges and four universities that were designed to identify innovations that could be expanded to other schools and improve student outcomes. The board says the projects centered on "robust advising and monitoring systems, offering adult learning options with paths to career and college, and providing accelerated models such as modular, non-course based, and integrated course options to accelerate a student's pathway toward degree attainment" (Texas Higher Education Coordinating Board, 2012, p. 2). The specific goal was to boost completion rates among developmental education students by improving programs while providing the state with an opportunity to promote systemic reform. As part of a Statewide Developmental Education plan, the coordinating board has adopted this goal: "By fall 2017, Texas will significantly improve the success of underprepared students by addressing their individualized needs through reliable diagnostic assessment, comprehensive support services, and nontraditional interventions, to include modular, mainstreaming, non-course competency-based, technologically-based, and integrated instructional models" (Texas Higher Education Coordinating Board, 2013). Clearly,

Texas is very aggressively addressing the critical issue of improving developmental education outcomes.

Efforts to Improve: The SOAR Institute

Alabama is not among the states that have attempted to reform developmental education on a systemwide level, though there are some excellent programs at individual schools. Soon after I arrived at Shelton State in 2008, I knew developmental education programming had to change. This narrative recounts how we restructured developmental education programming, providing an account of how one school launched a comprehensive effort to improve developmental education outcomes, using the most effective approaches we could identify. Once the decision had been made to take the plunge, I did what educators are prone to do: I formed a study group. Actually, it operated more like a task force of concerned faculty and staff members who were genuinely interested in improving the fortunes of the underprepared student population. We examined the pass rates and quickly came to the conclusion that radical changes were needed to improve outcomes in our developmental education program. The team comprised instructors from developmental English and developmental mathematics, a reading faculty representative, the director of the Adult Education program, the retention officer, a representative from advising, and the director of special projects.

In the fall of 2009, the team began devising a comprehensive plan to address the critical needs of Shelton State's developmental education students. The team's charter was to study successful developmental education programs in Alabama and elsewhere, identify best practices, and propose a plan that would bring improvements. Early on, the team held four brainstorming sessions that were open to faculty and staff with one session dedicated specifically to the counseling staff. Team members hit the road to visit other colleges to discuss what was working in well-performing developmental education programs and to get a firsthand look at successful tutoring centers, learning labs, and so on. Visits were made to Pellissippi State Community College in Knoxville, Tennessee; Tallahassee Community College in Tallahassee, Florida; Wallace State Community College–Hanceville in Hanceville, Alabama; Northeast Alabama Community College in Rainsville, Alabama; and Hinds Community College in Raymond, Mississippi. The team held telephone conference calls with officials at Northwest Vista Community College in San Antonio, Texas, and Valencia College in Orlando, Florida. All the bases were touched in an effort to identify the elements needed for the overhaul.

After about six months of work, the structure of the redesigned developmental education program had taken shape:

- A director would be installed to oversee the three major components of the program: instructional, advising, and tutoring.
- As part of the instructional component, faculty members would be appointed math and reading coordinators, all of whom would work with the director and their division chairs.
- The advising component involved the creation of specialized advisor positions called "Navigators," who would be assigned to students once they were placed in developmental education. Navigators had the critical role of providing both guidance and encouragement.
- Under the tutoring component, *all* students, whether enrolled in developmental education courses or not, would have access to professional tutors. Currently under development are high-touch, professionally staffed, dedicated labs for students in reading, writing, and math, which will open soon and be available for all students, not just those in developmental education, removing a stigma.
- The project soon received an official name—the SOAR Institute, or Student Opportunities for Achievement and Resources—and developed its mission, which explicitly called for the program to "provide dedicated support to enhance the success of underprepared students." Dr. Hunter Boylan spent two days at Shelton State during the early planning phase, providing insight and advice; he remains plugged into the program's progress and today is considered an advisor and guide.

Dr. Boylan's ideas have served as the foundation of the SOAR Institute. Boylan and his colleagues have identified many of the elements that help increase successful developmental education outcomes, and many of those components were baked into the redesign. For instance, we wanted to provide comprehensive support services to students to boost their chances for success, noting that "tutoring, advising and instructional programs with a strong professional development component had greater rates of student retention and better performance in developmental courses than programs without such an emphasis" (Boylan, Bonham, Claxton, & Bliss, 1992). At Shelton State, we made sure that the tutoring delivered at the SOAR Institute would be delivered by well-trained tutors; each tutor receives a minimum of 10 hours of training, a portion of which is addressed through a program called "Developmental Education 101," where they learn how to talk to underprepared students and respond to their learning styles as well as how to develop effective teaching tactics and assessment techniques. Each tutor trainee also receives preparation spelled out by the Association for Tutoring Professionals in conjunction with requirements for tutor program certification through ITTPC, the International Tutor Training Program Certification. Because the SOAR Institute tutors *all* students, training is not solely focused on developmental students. A SOAR Tutor Supervisor was hired to oversee the day-to-day operations of the school's tutoring service, and the tutoring staff was expanded to include more than 25 tutors, available to all students from 7:30 a.m. until 7:30 p.m. daily. (An online tutoring service is accessible around the clock.)

The instruction of developmental courses also received attention. First, we set a goal of assigning more full-time faculty members to teach developmental courses. To cite just one example, Shelton State had only one full-time instructor teaching MTH 090 in 2007; by 2011, that figure had increased to four. Second, we increased opportunities for staff training and professional development for those working with students in developmental education courses. In 2011–12, a dozen professional development sessions on five different topics were offered to full-time faculty members as well as adjunct instructors. Finally, an instructional redesign was launched to examine new ways to teach foundational courses, which is discussed later.

As the revamped developmental education program's contours came into focus, the advising component—renamed "Navigator"—took on a new, intrusive quality. Before the overhaul of the developmental education program, students at Shelton State did not have assigned advisors, thus depriving them of a crucial relationship at a time many of them were facing difficult academic challenges. The Navigator program, with its aggressive approach, swung the needle in the other direction. Three Navigators were hired for the debut of the SOAR Institute. All of them received comprehensive training before the program launched in the fall of 2011 (the number of Navigators has since doubled). As the name suggests, Shelton State's Navigators are not passive advisors for the community college's underprepared students but, rather, a combination of mentor/life coach/cheerleader. They have been called "advisors on steroids."

When our redesign was being planned, the team members gave the advising component careful thought, recalling that during their inspection trips to other community colleges' developmental education programs, they always received recommendations to include effective advising services to help underprepared students. Once the hiring process began, particular attention was paid to selecting the people who would act as Navigators. Advising services typically are among the lowest ranked of all the support services provided at colleges and universities, so it was essential to secure the right individuals in those roles if this aspect of the program was going to work as intended. Personnel choices are never scientific and often hard to explain, but we wanted personalities who could push students normally resistant to encouragement, gradually instilling in those students a sense of accountability for their own academic success.

With an initial roster of just three, it was clear that we could not assign a Navigator to every student enrolled in a developmental education course. So we decided that the Navigators would be assigned to students placed in at least two developmental education courses. Each first-term Navigator received 30–40 students, with more added during the second term. Another key feature of the Navigator program was that these specialized advisors would be introduced early in the first-time student's college career—immediately, in fact, after the assessment results that placed them in developmental education.

Early Intervention Is Key

Research shows that early intervention is critical for underprepared students: Failure at the first level of developmental education can spell doom for many students, locking them into a cycle of struggle and frustration that often causes them to give up and quit school. At Shelton State, we practice early intervention techniques. Within our existing programs, the Navigators make contact with their assigned student before classes begin, establishing a relationship that becomes a resource for the student. In a follow-up meeting, Navigators outline the program and the school's resources, discuss time management strategies, and emphasize student responsibilities. To foster open communication between the student and the Navigator, the student signs a "contract" that defines clear objectives and outlines expectations. As part of this pact, the student pledges to meet with the Navigator on a regular basis, provide the specialized advisor with an overview of assignments for each class, and submit a goal-setting worksheet and an academic progress report, among other things. At the same time, the Navigator builds a profile of the student, inquiring about his or her academic strengths and weaknesses, ambitions and obligations, as well as resources. After the initial contact, the Navigators monitor progress and meet regularly with their students, sometimes weekly with the students at highest risk, but most commonly they meet every other week. Navigators are apprised when their students fail to show up for class or stumble on assignments. It is not uncommon for them to pick up the phone to call one of their students if an issue has emerged. At the same time, Navigators are there to send a congratulatory message if that is in order.

For the student, the message broadcast by the establishment of the SOAR Institute is clear: Shelton State cares about your success—and cares enough to create an extensive support system to make sure you can succeed. This was not lip service; the investment in this initiative has been substantial, as was the work to execute it.

Program Success and Future Outlook

In just one year, the SOAR Institute became one of Shelton State's largest departments, with 11 full-time staff members and 35 part-time staffers. The institute itself was placed in a prime campus location with new furnishings. A newsletter, called *SOARing*, was launched, and twice weekly student success seminars such as "Study Tips and Note-Taking Strategies" and "Student Survival Kit" were held on campus. In response, demand for tutoring services through the SOAR Institute hit a new high. During the first week of class in August 2011, the SOAR Institute served 1,088 students, a figure that rose to 1,289 students and 218 tutoring sessions during the second week. In the fall of 2011, students in math courses received nearly 1,100 hours of assistance, while those in English courses received more than 475 hours. When the hours of tutoring services students received from other courses are included, the total becomes 1,830 hours. In the fall of 2012, the SOAR Institute had contact with an average of 135 students using its services each day, with another 42 students taking advantage of tutoring, a total of 186 daily contacts on average.

The SOAR Institute's early results strongly suggest that improvements are being realized. As of spring 2013, a total of 913 Shelton State students have met with or been advised by a SOAR Institute Navigator. The first full year of the program has seen higher pass rates in developmental education courses for students with Navigators than for the average of all students in the courses. In the fall of 2011, the first semester of the SOAR Institute, 50.7% of students with a Navigator passed their developmental education courses, compared with 41.4% for all students in those courses. In the spring of 2012, the pattern was repeated, as 46% of students with a Navigator passed their developmental education courses, compared with 38.2% overall. (These rates also are an improvement over the three-year averages for the fall and spring semesters mentioned earlier.)

With the SOAR Institute in place, persistence rates also showed improvement at Shelton State. In the fall of 2011, the percentage of students with a Navigator who finished their developmental education coursework was 81.5%, compared with 76.6% of students overall. In the spring of 2012, the percentage of Navigator-assisted students who finished their developmental education courses was 84.1%, compared with the 75.2% overall rate. Progression to all college-level classes also has been rising since the debut of the SOAR Institute. In the spring of 2012, the rate was 12%; it increased to 38% in the fall of 2012 and to 59% in the spring of 2013. The retention rate for Navigator-assisted students (41% in the spring of 2013) is much higher than the overall rate for Shelton State (10%). In an interview at Shelton State, Velissa, a student who resumed her academic career after a long absence from the classroom, offered this assessment of the SOAR Institute: "Even if I had not placed in those lower classes, I would have wanted to be part of that as well. With being out of school so long, you have the resources to help you accomplish those goals. Help with classes, books, computers, and you can go and talk to someone about things you are going through."

That is only one student's view. The true test will be whether this kind of improvement can be sustained over the long term, and, if that is the case, whether it can be scaled as part of a broader overhaul of developmental education programs in the Alabama Community College System. I believe the early results at Shelton State to be very encouraging, but careful evaluation of SOAR Institute data is needed. In the meantime, the SOAR Institute is moving forward with additional improvements. An intense review of how developmental education courses are taught began in 2012, with significant course redesigns planned, beginning with mathematics courses. Two full-time mathematics faculty members have been named course captains, and they have been meeting with the math division chair and the SOAR Institute director to study options for the redesign, with a goal of launching the revised program in the fall of 2014. The team is looking at redesigned programs at other institutions, and plans call for a modular approach to instruction so that students can move through developmental math more quickly. (Modularized courses generally allow students to show mastery through a series of short, focused assessments, and once they demonstrate proficiency, they can move on to more advanced modules.) A basic study skills course is being continually evaluated and updated. Collaboration with the school's adult education program is continuing, aimed at aggressively assisting another segment of the underprepared population. Future plans include the establishment of an advisory committee for the program and the addition of designated labs for mathematics, writing, and reading, staffed with lab assistants. Supplemental instruction components are planned for designated courses. The SOAR Institute intends to offer "boot camps" for students who place within three points of the cut score in Compass® assessment testing and aims to assist with the development of a bridge program for high school students to prepare them for Compass testing, improve their study skills, and better prepare them for the academic challenges of college life. Significantly, there are hopes that the Navigator program can be expanded so that every Shelton State student who places in a single developmental education course can benefit from that promising program.

Although the student response to the SOAR Institute has been positive, predictably there has been resistance from some Shelton State faculty members who believe the resources devoted to the program should have gone elsewhere. At every institution, there are faculty who sincerely believe in a "sink-or-swim" philosophy when it comes to student success; they see it as a way of selecting those who truly deserve the privilege of a college education. And, of course, there is one factor that is rarely mentioned in the debate over developmental education: cost. A 2008 study estimated the annual cost of remediation in the United States at between $1.9 billion and $2.3 billion at community colleges, and another $500 million at four-year colleges (Bailey, 2009). There also is a high cost for students who end up in these courses, both financially and sometimes psychologically. To pay for these noncredit courses, students have to spend their own money, accumulate debt, or tap into limited financial aid packages. The additional time spent in developmental education classes can delay their progress toward a credential or degree, which has been shown to be a factor in reducing the likelihood of completion (Horn & Nevill, 2006).

So the question becomes: Is it worth it? I prefer to view the flip side of this equation and weigh the expenditure of those resources against the loss of human capital that would occur had we not taken that path to dramatically restructure developmental education at Shelton State. Helping underprepared students get on the right track can change the destiny of a family, triggering a positive domino effect that can raise an Alabama resident from a dismal future of low-wage jobs to employment in an automotive assembly plant with annual earnings exceeding $75,000.

Yes, there are serious concerns about how developmental education is currently structured, but that does not change the fact that a large percentage of students arrive at community colleges simply unprepared to do college-level work, making some form of assistance necessary. The issue then becomes how it is delivered. I mentioned earlier a statement made by researcher Charles Claxton—"Bad remediation costs about as much as good remediation" (Boylan & Saxon, 2005, p. 9)—and it bears repeating because it is so true. Now more than ever, resources devoted to developmental education in community colleges should be deployed effectively. This realization should trigger a sense of urgency as developmental education redesign is considered, given that we cannot afford to waste resources at a time when community colleges are being called on to shoulder more of the nation's important workforce development duties. As policymakers, administrators, and educators, we must get this right.

References

Bailey, T. (2009). *Rethinking developmental education in community college.* Community College Research Center, CCRC Brief, Number 40 [Data file]. Retrieved from http://www.ccaurora.edu/ssrd/5/5-20_rethinking_development_education _in_community_college.pdf

Boylan, H., Bonham, B., Claxton C., and Bliss, L. (1992). *The state of the art in developmental education: Report of a national study.* Paper presented at the First National Conference on Research in Developmental Education, Charlotte, NC.

Boylan, H. R., & Saxon, D. P. (2005). *What works in remediation: Lessons from 30 years of research.* National Center for Developmental Education paper prepared for the League for Innovation in the Community College [Data file.] Retrieved from http://inpathways.net/Boylan--What%20Works.pdf

Charles A. Dana Center, Complete College America, Inc., Education Commission of the States, & Jobs for the Future (2012). *Core principles for transforming remedial education: A joint statement* [Data file]. Retrieved from http://www .completecollege.org/docs/Remediation_Joint_Statement-Embargo.pdf

Horn, L., & Nevill, S. (2006). *Profile of undergraduates in U.S. postsecondary education institutions, 2003–4: With a special analysis of community college students.* Washington, DC: U.S. Department of Education, National Center for Education Statistics.

Kelley, D. B., & Murphy, L. J. (2006). *100% Math Initiative: Building a foundation for student success in developmental mathematics.* Developmental Math Professionals, Community College System of Massachusetts [Data file]. Retrieved from http://www.masscc.org/sites/massc.drupalgardens.com/files/mathinitiativefinal .pdf

Massachusetts Community College Executive Office. (2006). *100% Math Initiative: Building a foundation for student success in developmental mathematics* [Data file]. Retrieved from http://www.masscc.org/sites/massc.drupalgardens.com/files/ mathinitiativefinal.pdf

Sperling, C. B. (2009). *Access and quality: Improving the performance of Massachusetts community college developmental education programs.* Massachusetts Community College Developmental Education Best Practice and Policy Audit [Data file]. Retrieved from http://www.masscc.org/sites/massc.drupalgardens.com/files/ accessandquality.pdf

Texas Higher Education Coordinating Board. (2012, March). *Overview: Transforming developmental education.* Retrieved from http://www.thecb.state.tx.us/download

.cfm?downloadfile=D7A43E20-9FAA-1EA9-7415ADBA401CB9E4&typename
=dmFile&fieldname=filename

Texas Higher Education Coordinating Board. (2013). *Developmental Education/
Texas Success Initiative.* Retrieved from http://www.thecb.state.tx.us/index
.cfm?objectid=233A17D9-F3D3-BFAD-D5A76CDD8AADD1E3

6

LESSONS ON LEADERSHIP

K–12 Dropout Prevention Models in Promoting Postsecondary Education Success

Steve Dobo

Every great dream begins with a dreamer.

—Harriet Tubman

I was not seen for who I was while growing up. That has been one of the driving forces in my life. I used to think I was different because of this fact, but I have come to find my situation to be the norm. Parents do the best they can to see and encourage their children, and my parents did better than most at encouraging me. Some say that one's deepest wound presents itself as the greatest gift to the world. In my case, this wound has evolved into my purpose in the world: seeing the potential in all young people and creating avenues, pathways, and systems to assist them in actualizing their potential.

I am absolutely inspired by the remarkable capability of youth. I unequivocally believe in the potential for all students to achieve success in education and life. In the United States, we are not struggling with a "dropout crisis," from which you would infer that the problem stems from the personal deficiencies of our young people. Rather, we are experiencing a "dropout system problem," which is an unintended result of a 100-year-old educational factory system model built for a different purpose in a different time. With approximately 50% of our urban students of color and poverty dropping out of school, it is not really about deficiencies in our students, but about the dysfunction of our educational system. We can do better—we can create a system that creates multiple pathways for every single young person to have a customized road to success in education and life. Special education had it right in creating Individualized Education Programs for students—and should serve as a model to extend that individualized attention to all students.

Our disenfranchised youth often appear as the character of Pig-Pen in the *Peanuts* comic strip, that is, walking around with a cloud of dust and debris behind them. The world tends to focus on the cloud of dust, but I have always been more interested in seeing the person inside that cloud. To give an example, I often reference the movie *Avatar*. In the movie, the Na'vi race live within a culture of understanding based on recognizing each other for who they appear to be from the inside rather than judging from the outside. Specifically, when they greet each other, they say, "I see you," and the other responds in turn with "I see you." I am committed to creating systems that see young people for all the potential that lies within them.

The purpose of this chapter is to explore the implications of the dropout reduction work I embarked upon over the years in founding Colorado Youth for a Change. I also specifically highlight the insights of the Aurora Futures Academy model on community college practices in helping General Education Development (GED®) completers become more successful as they navigate the postsecondary education system.

Colorado Youth for a Change

Many years ago, I worked at Urban Peak in Denver, Colorado, assisting the numerous disenfranchised of our youth by creating educational programs for homeless teenagers. The program, designed to empower homeless youth, consisted of a GED Preparation Program (GED Lab) just eight feet from where 40 homeless youth slept every night. Most of our young people took advantage of this program, and I made a point to host end-of-the-year heart-felt ceremonies celebrating their successes. Relatives would come out of the woodwork to recognize one of the first educational achievements these youth had accomplished. Everyone would clap and cry, but one thing always stuck in my heart: This was going to be the educational terminus for most of these students.

Over the years I worked at Urban Peak, very few GED completers were able to go on to community college and pass a single college course. Most who enrolled ended up being placed in remedial-level classes and languishing there before becoming frustrated and dropping out of college. Most expended all of their available time, energy, and finances. More important, they expended their hope and perseverance and never took (much less passed) a credit-bearing class. Periodically, we heard of the "canary in the coal mine" GED student who did happen to figure it out on his or her own and earn an associate's degree, then a bachelor's degree, and was later seeking a master's. So it could be done, but the systems and processes were not in place for that to be a common occurrence. I vowed then that I would someday create a program that would help students obtain a GED and go on to become successful at a community college.

I soon left Urban Peak and founded a nonprofit organization called Colorado Youth for a Change (CYC). The mission of this organization was to help solve Colorado's high school dropout crisis. At the time, Colorado had more than 18,000 students dropping out of school annually. CYC adopted then governor Bill Ritter's campaign goal of cutting the dropout rate in half within 10 years. Jumping into the black hole of the dropout crisis, we formulated a three-pronged strategy involving dropout recovery, dropout intervention, and new school program creation.

Dropout recovery involved partnerships with school districts in which CYC was contracted to reach out to students who had dropped out, address the challenges they had in returning to school, help them explore schools in which to re-enroll, and provide follow-up services for a year to ensure retention in their school placement. Today, after eight years of operation, CYC works with seven Colorado school districts and helps more than 550 dropout students return to school each year. Seventy-five percent of these students are still in school after their first year back.

We knew that we would never solve the dropout crisis unless we could get ahead of the curve; waiting till students dropped out was the end of the line. We looked for research to indicate where and when we should intervene in the K–12 curriculum to prevent high school dropout behavior. The University of Chicago Consortium on Chicago School Research had just published "What Matters for Staying On-Track and Graduating in Chicago Public High Schools" in July 2007 (Allensworth & Easton, 2007); this report identified ninth grade as a key time for intervention and course failures as the key indicator. CYC created its ninth-grade intervention program based on this research and now has 10 intervention specialists working with ninth graders to prevent course failure in 11 high schools across five Colorado school districts. We developed a conceptual framework based on the reasons that ninth graders fail classes and developed an intervention tool kit of research-based strategies for CYC intervention specialists to use in working with students. Using the initial grade reports in the semester in ninth grade as the baseline, CYC currently helps 75% of ninth graders with one to two course failures on record raise their grades to passing by the end of each semester. According to Chicago research, passing more of their classes in ninth grade gives them a much better probability of staying on track to a four-year, on-time graduation.

With dropout recovery, CYC outreach specialists were often finding students who wanted to return to school, but there were no open seats in school programs that were a good fit for them and sometimes no existing programs to meet their needs. CYC soon grew into the business of creating new school programs for returning dropouts to enroll in that were customized to their exact needs. Since then, CYC has created six school programs with partnering school districts over the last eight years and currently operates Aurora Futures Academy in partnership with Aurora Public Schools.

Based on these efforts, the most recently available school data for the 2011–12 school year reveals that Colorado, in a five-year period, has achieved a 32% reduction in the raw number of dropouts. Various CYC partner school districts have witnessed an even more impressive reduction in dropout numbers, with Denver Public Schools realizing a 45% reduction, Englewood Schools achieving a 59% reduction, and Boulder Valley School District experiencing a remarkable 68% reduction. CYC is ahead of schedule on its way to helping Colorado meet Governor Bill Ritter's challenge of cutting the dropout rate in half within 10 years.

Aurora Futures Academy

After founding CYC, I began looking for a school district that would implement the GED Plus program that I had envisioned while working with teens at the homeless shelter. CYC, which had helped recruit the initial student body to open up a new blended learning school program, was developing a great partnership with Aurora Public Schools (APS). We started looking at data and showing the APS administration that there were a significant number of students who had dropped out each of the past three years who were too far behind and too old to recover for a high school diploma program. APS was intrigued with the idea of creating a school program that would help dropouts return to school to prepare for the GED, enroll in career-technical industry certificate programs, and attend community college. In the 2009–10 school year, APS and CYC partnered in creating Aurora Futures Academy for 100 previous dropouts to return to school.

Key Program Elements

Prior to developing the Futures program, I spent years identifying the main reasons why most GED completers do not persist to the postsecondary level, not to mention theorizing about the program elements to be developed for the purpose of realizing different and better results. The following sections discuss the program elements that I have found to be key to the success of Aurora Futures Academy.

Funding
GED programs in Colorado are mostly drop-in programs inadequately and unsustainably funded through grants. We developed an alternative source of funding that would allow us sufficient resources to create an actual school with robust direct instruction by highly qualified teachers. In so doing, we found that we could structure a GED program so that GED students could continue to take high school–accredited courses but have a different course of study with the different goal of obtaining a GED rather than a diploma. In that way, school districts would continue to garner the state-funded per-pupil operating amount for each of our GED students, and CYC could negotiate with APS for 75% of that funding to operate Aurora Futures Academy.

Instruction
With enough money to fund robust direct instruction, we tailored the program to meet the exact needs of our students in returning to school to obtain their GEDs and bridge to postsecondary community college and career-technical programs. We hired experienced language arts and mathematics instructors who were highly qualified and worked with APS to create the curriculum for school district–certified course titles. With the classes Pre-Collegiate Language Arts and Pre-Collegiate Mathematics, teachers tailor the direct instruction to mirror the methodology and techniques that students will experience at the college level. Staff strive to build a college culture in all of their conversations, classrooms, and advising office, but sometimes, because of student attendance and student needs, instructors have to individualize instruction or lessons for a student so that he or she can walk away with something for that day.

School District Partnership
Aurora Futures Academy operates as a contract school program and can exist only if it is in a strong partnership with a school district. APS generously donates space at Pickens Technical College to operate the program, provides free access to 39 career-technical programs, and includes Futures students within its concurrent enrollment agreement, so that Futures students can take courses at the Community College of Aurora (CCA) free of charge, which are designated as transferable to a four-year degree program.

Individual Future Plans
Students who enroll in Futures often have not found success at previous traditional high school or alternative school programs. Some of our students

come to us having passed no classes at high school over a number of years and are now between the ages of 17 and 20. One of the keys to the success of Futures is in working with each student to identify individual goals and an individual plan to reach those goals. Students choose how long they want to stay in the program, picking from all or a subset of goals including becoming a GED completer, earning one or more career-technical industry certificates, or even taking community college courses up to earning an associate's degree.

College and Careers Class

One of the requirements for students who enroll in Futures is to express a desire and an intention not only to finish the GED credential, but to go on to career-technical college or community college. However, students often arrive at Futures without the soft skills to be successful in their current and future education. Futures student advisors and Goodwill Industries staff co-developed and co-teach a college and careers course to provide the soft skills for educational and career success. Students learn organizational, time-management, goal-setting, decision-making, and study skills along with the basics of financial aid and faculty expectations at the college level, specifically geared toward the CCA and Pickens options. This class is an in-house version of the Community College 101 class but is taught on the Futures campus by Futures instructors.

Support, Support, and More Support

One of the major keys to student success involves the extensive support provided by Futures advisors, with a low ratio of one advisor for every 60 students. Such a ratio allows for advisors to devote the time and energy toward building supportive relationships with their students. Upon meeting with students for the first time, advisors address any barriers that the student may have to his or her educational success, such as transportation, health problems, mental health issues, substance use, housing, working, and caring for children. Advisors provide help to students directly and identify outside support programs to connect students right away in order to address these pressing issues. Furthermore, advisors serve as the students' chief cheerleaders, recognizing accomplishments, encouraging students during difficult times, and giving a gentle nudge when needed.

College Readiness and Enrollment

When students are identified as college-ready, they are given the opportunity to take either career-technical programs at Pickens Technical College or classes at CCA. The criteria considered for these opportunities are attendance,

Futures grades and academic performance, scores on the Test of Adult Basic Education (TABE), Accuplacer or ACT scores, the ability to take and pass at least one section of the GED test, the Individual Career and Academic Plan (ICAP), and staff recommendations. At this point, they are assigned to the Futures college advisor and are enrolled in a special section of the College and Careers course taught by this same advisor. Students who need extra preparation or are especially excited to begin classes on a college campus are then enrolled in the CCA College 101 course, in which they learn their way around campus, connect with all of the available support services, and learn more about college expectations. Being on the campus and conceptualizing themselves for the first time as college students is transformative for these students. Futures students take this class as a cohort and return to the Futures campus after the class to collectively debrief as a group and finish course assignments. Through this cohort- and counselor-supported approach, we have started to determine the high level of support from the Futures staff that students need in order to be successful at college.

Bridging to College Academic Courses
One of the major goals of Aurora Futures Academy is to prepare students, while they are still in the K–12 system, to complete the Accuplacer college placement test and place out of the remedial series of classes and into credit-bearing college classes. Once students take College 101 on the CCA campus, and place into credit-bearing class levels through the Accuplacer, they can sign up to take free classes at CCA. The same cohort approach is used here as in the College 101 class, in which the Futures college counselor is assigned to lead group study sessions for all CCA students on the Futures campus daily after class. In addition to these services, Futures has a college liaison who meets with students on the CCA campus, serves as a liaison to college instructors, and connects students to needed support services on the CCA campus. Through this approach, Futures is helping more and more students become successful at the college level.

Implications for Community Colleges

The experiences that we have garnered in running Aurora Futures Academy for the last four years have provided much needed insight on retention components that can work effectively at the community college level. The following sections provide recommendations for community college personnel to consider in order to foster success, educate, and guide students with GED credentials through the postsecondary education process.

Robust GED Prep Instruction

GED prep instruction occurs in many different forms in different institutions across the United States. Community colleges have an opportunity to take the lead in creating more robust instructional methodology and techniques for GED preparation that mirrors the instructional environment students will face at the college level. By modeling a deliberate attempt to bridge GED students to postsecondary education, community colleges can set a new bar for local nonprofits and K–12 school systems for the standards of what an effective GED program should look like at the postsecondary level. With the changes in the GED being tied more closely to the common core standards in January 2014, there is a need for more thorough instruction in all GED prep programs. Providing more opportunities for GED prep students to enroll in college classes while concurrently preparing for the GED is also a good way for students to land a foothold in their future academic environment.

Linkages to K–12 School Systems and Nonprofit Organizations

Because community colleges do not represent the totality of institutions involved in GED preparation, it would be valuable for them to link partnership with the local K–12 school systems and community-based organizations for the purpose of smoothing the transition from GED to college. Community colleges can better inform these GED prep programs of the expectations that college faculty will have of their students, as well as some of the instructional and soft skills supports that are to be provided to students to help them be better prepared for college. Community college representatives should visit the GED prep programs and host tours and site visits for GED students to visit the individual community college campuses.

Proactive Support

GED students often attempt to fly under the radar, so it is important for community colleges to be proactive in identifying and supporting these students early on in their collegiate careers. From our experience with Aurora Futures Academy, we found that it does not take very long for these students to fall behind in attendance, assignments, or grades, and then disappear. Supportive relationships with college support personnel need to be established before classes start, so that if students quickly encounter difficulties, they will feel comfortable seeking out college staff for support. Students ideally will feel so accustomed to accessing the college support systems that it will be their natural tendency to reach out if they encounter difficulty.

GED Cohorts

Providing students the opportunity to take classes with a cohort of students with similar experiences eases their transition into the community college environment. In providing the cohort experience, students are able to sit together in class, share class notes, complete projects together, remind each other of assignments due, and study for tests in groups. This gives students a natural group of first friends at the college level, not to mention the chance to share with others their academic strengths while relying on others to help them in areas of academic weakness. When students are given the opportunity to meet with others of similar academic backgrounds, they become better equipped to transition more smoothly when enrolling in other collegiate-level coursework.

Instructors

For GED prep programs delivered on community college campuses, instructors must serve to bridge the GED and college classes by teaching a selection of both types of coursework. Ideally, these instructors should be selected from the strongest in the university, both proficient and creative in the academic areas they teach, and strong in building supportive and nurturing relationships with students who are at risk. Instructors may also be grouped together to teach a cohort of GED students, similar to (K–12) ninth-grade academies, which share data and information as to how students are doing across the spectrum of shared academic classes. Rather than being at the low end of the totem pole, these instructor positions should be the most highly prized and rewarded. We need our best instructors to be the first experience our GED students have while attending college.

College 101

College 101 is an excellent class for all GED students to take to launch their college careers. Community colleges must consider scheduling these classes in a block format so that cohorts of GED students enroll as a learning community. College 101 can be expanded to a semester-long course that involves career assessment and career development, organizational and time-management skills, self-advocacy, academic tutoring, and connection to social-emotional supports both on and off campus. Such coursework lays the groundwork for GED students to gain the necessary soft skills to succeed in a more rigorous college environment. Offering current GED students the opportunity to visit college classes, become involved in college clubs and activities, and access college support services will also help to prepare them for the initial experience of college enrollment.

Individual Plans

Comprehensive advising is essential for GED students to launch a successful college career and persist to graduation. The advising function for these students needs to be expanded to include not only help with the registration process, but in-depth assistance in understanding college majors and career choice, as well as preparing for life after college. Helping students understand where college fits within the context of their lives is essential to keeping students on track when difficulties arise. Advisors should use the K–12 concept of an ICAP to pull all of this information together at the beginning of a student's college career, and then revisit it periodically to revise and evaluate student progress toward key goals.

Conclusion

GED students have immense potential to succeed but will need tighter collaboration between K–12 and college systems, along with greater support and alterations to traditional ways of doing business. Aurora Futures Academy is one example of a program that is demonstrating that GED students can be successful at the postsecondary level within the community college and career-technical college. Elements of the Futures Academy model should be used as examples for GED Plus programs operating at the community college level that bridge GED preparation to college-level courses. These elements have the potential to increase enrollment of GED completers, as well as raise their persistence levels toward completion of industry certificates, associate's degrees, and bachelor's degrees. In addition, community colleges will find that this additional attention and support not only is necessary at the point of transition from K–12, but really represents a new standard of practice to be adopted for the GED students' entire stay at the community college.

Reference

Allensworth, E. M., & Easton, J. Q. (2007, July). *What matters for staying on-track and graduating in Chicago public high schools.* Chicago, IL: University of Chicago Consortium on Chicago School Research.

7

DELVING INTO THE TRENCHES

A Practitioner's Perspective

Pamela Blumenthal

A teacher affects eternity; he can never tell where his influence stops.

—Henry B. Adams

Like many of our students, Ananda (see Profile 1) felt that coming to Portland Community College (PCC) Prep Alternative Programs was her last chance for academic success. Over the years, I have heard this same sentiment expressed again and again. Often students reach us as the last stop in a long road of failure. They have been deemed "not college material" by people and systems along the way and have come to believe it. Each student who comes to us has a unique story and a desire to change his or her path, but the students don't know where to start. We are here to help them rewrite their stories. For many students, a General Education Development (GED®) certificate is part of that story; the first chapter on their way to academic success. At PCC Prep Alternative Programs, we become the network of support for students until they can stand on their own. Many of our students don't come to us believing they can succeed. It is our job to believe in them from the start—until we are able to convince them to believe in themselves.

Profile 1

When Ananda started in our Gateway to College program she possessed strong academic skills. Still, her struggles with drug addiction and other social and emotional challenges eventually caused her to drop out of the program. After several weeks in rehab, and finding a new focus on her health, Ananda entered our Youth Empowered to Succeed (YES) program. She completed her GED in one term. Ananda, 21, then returned to PCC's nationally recognized Gateway to College program and completed her high school diploma and credits toward an associate of science degree. She is interested in pursuing a career in nutrition. In her academic journey Ananda has experienced many ups and downs, but earning her GED was one important step on her path forward.

Focusing on Groundbreaking Models for Student Success

Our mission at PCC to serve at-risk high school students began almost 20 years ago. PCC Prep Alternative Programs started with one program providing vocational English as a Second Language (ESL) to new immigrants. Today, we are a department of five programs serving an array of student needs. We annually work with more than 1,800 students in our high school and college programs. Our department's goal has always been to support underserved populations, and our services continue to evolve with students' needs as the main focus.

Gateway to College

In 2000, several creative, innovative professionals, led by the vision of then-director Linda Huddle, developed the Gateway to College dropout recovery model. Gateway is designed to help students who have dropped out of high school or are not on track to graduate and prepare them for college classes through an intensive learning community. In Gateway, students take college courses and earn both college and high school credit. Many of our graduates end up close to earning an associate's degree when they complete their high school diploma. Through an intensive support model, these students (of whom many in their lives had given up on them) develop confidence and competence in Gateway. In 2003, the Bill and Melinda Gates Foundation provided PCC with a grant to replicate our program. Today, Gateway to College exists in 43 community colleges in 23 states. The Gateway to College

National Network is a successful nonprofit organization, bringing this model to colleges around the country.

Gateway to College is a wonderful option for many students, but it is not the complete answer for addressing dropout recovery. We have a significant number of students for whom a high school diploma is not an option. Some students are overage and under credit and unlikely to be able to obtain a high school diploma. The GED is necessary for providing not only a completion but also a fresh start for entry into college or a career.

YES Program

In our YES program we serve approximately 600 students ages 16–21 annually. Our students often arrive with multiple barriers to academic success. Unlike Gateway to College students, YES students are more likely to be living on their own, working, and supporting a family. They often require in-depth remediation due to past issues with attendance and low academic skills. They are more likely to have received special education services and to have struggled with behavioral issues and/or drugs and alcohol. The YES program also supports a significant number of English Language Learners (ELLs). Our third high school program, the Multicultural Academic Program (MAP), provides a bridge for students who need intensive English language acquisition. After achieving high English proficiency, students can enter either YES or Gateway. Because many of our ELL students are older with fewer credits, the GED offered through YES is a better fit for their circumstances.

Our high school programs are funded through annual contracts with seven school districts in the Portland area. We receive state funding to retrieve dropouts and help support students toward completion of a high school diploma or GED credential. Without such intervention, many of these students would otherwise fall through the cracks. These partnerships provide a win-win situation for both PCC and the districts.

Our array of programs allows us to serve at-risk students with varied needs and strengths. Each student comes with a unique story and differing needs. Having multiple programs in our department allows flexibility and choice for students. It is empowering for students to be able to choose how to move forward with their education. If the schedule and requirements of Gateway turn out to be too much for a student, he or she can transfer into our YES GED program. When a student increases his or her English literacy in our MAP program, that student can then decide whether Gateway or YES is the best next step.

Our success and expertise with working with at-risk high school students has given us the foundation to create two new programs: Future Connect and Project Degree. Both of these programs provide at-risk GED and high school graduates with support and opportunities as they transition to college at PCC.

Future Connect

Staying in college and succeeding academically is a great challenge for students who have experienced minimal academic success. Like Tiffany (see Profile 2), many GED graduates enter college with low academic skills and life circumstances that make obtaining a college degree extremely difficult. One of our newest programs, Future Connect, was created to improve the odds for first-generation/low-income students. The personalized support from the coach is the key. Tiffany's coach, Dara, visited Tiffany's alternative school and got to know Tiffany as she was getting a GED. She provided information to students at that school about federal financial aid, college placement testing, and scholarships. Forming relationships with students in high schools and GED programs and maintaining those relationships when the students arrive at PCC creates deep bonds and helps set students up for success.

Profile 2

Tiffany was put in foster care at age 2. She bounced around for several years and lived with an abusive adoptive mom. When Tiffany got out of her abusive home at 14, she reconnected with her biological family and discovered that her family had experienced drug addiction and emotional abuse. Her brother encouraged her to complete her GED and go to college. She was awarded a scholarship in PCC's Future Connect Program in 2011. Since enrolling, Tiffany has received support from her coach, Dara. Through help and encouragement, she has excelled academically and personally. Tiffany now has her own apartment and last summer interned as an accounting assistant with the city of Portland. She has stayed on in that position part-time. Tiffany hopes to complete her associate's degree in accounting and obtain a job where she can support herself and continue to write the bright story of her future.

Future Connect is a partnership among PCC and three city governments in the Portland area. We provide scholarships and support to more than 500 low-income/first-generation students annually. In our unique funding model, the cities provide half of our cost and the PCC Foundation generates the other half through grants and donations. We are entering our third year and are already seeing extremely positive outcomes. In our first year we had a fall-to-fall retention rate of 70%. A typical retention rate for low-income/ first-generation students at PCC had been about 20%.

Project Degree

We find that many GED graduates enter college needing remediation. Approximately 25% of our Future Connect students enter college below college level, and the first courses they must take are in developmental education. Tiffany was one of these students. She started in our lowest-level courses in reading, writing, and math. We were able to enroll her in our Project Degree program, which is set up to provide extra support to students needing remediation. In Project Degree students take their courses as part of a learning community for their first two terms, and the curriculum for three classes is integrated. Attending classes with the same students for their first two terms builds a strong and supportive community. Service-learning is also part of the program, allowing students to experience practical applications for their coursework. The staff meets weekly so they can discuss students falling behind and devise plans to intervene. Project Degree was initially funded through a grant by the Gateway to College National Network. PCC is now supporting the program and evaluating ways that we might be able to expand upon our lessons learned to increase positive outcomes for students.

GED Is Essential to Postsecondary Access

Kyle (see Profile 3) did not complete a high school diploma, but because of his GED the door remains open for him to return to college. We know that high school graduates complete college at higher rates and earn more money than GED recipients. With this knowledge skeptics wonder why anyone would support GED programs. The reason is simple: One size does not fit all and it is essential to have multiple doors to academic success. Barriers and circumstances push and pull students out of traditional high schools. GED programs let students reengage in education and can give them skills to help them succeed. Many students feel hopeless after being expelled or failing out of school. Older students do not have the option of returning to high school. The flexibility and accessibility of the GED make it an important tool. Without it some populations would not have access to higher education.

The GED as an access point to college and careers is an issue of equity. In PCC Prep programs we see more Latino and African American students entering the YES program than in Gateway to College. The racial achievement gap that is prevalent in K–12 systems is perpetuated in community colleges. Students of color who have struggled in high school come to these colleges with lower test scores and drop out at higher rates. GED programs need to adopt culturally relevant pedagogy and practices in order to address educational inequity. We can make an impact on closing the gap, but we need to be conscious and deliberate in our actions.

Profile 3

Kyle stopped feeling connected to school in the sixth grade. He continued attending but dropped out just four months into his freshman year of high school. Academics came fairly easily to Kyle, especially math, but he had trouble seeing the relevance of what he was studying and he wanted to focus on his passion: music. Kyle found his way to our YES GED program when he was 16. He passed his GED tests in less than one term. Next he enrolled in Gateway to College to continue work toward his high school diploma and earn college credits, but he struggled with the college structure and did not have time to focus on music. He left Gateway, and now, at 24, Kyle continues to compose music and work. Some of his friends have moved on to careers and he wonders about his own next steps. Kyle is still committed to pursuing a career in music but is now considering taking a class or two to reengage in learning.

The reasons for dropping out are as varied as the students we support: Parents die. Children are put in foster care. Students develop chronic illnesses. There are students who live with drug or alcohol issues that make staying sober in high school impossible. Some are homeless; others are affected by gangs and are not safe in their neighborhood school. There are also academic and behavioral issues that can make meeting the requirements of a high school diploma extremely challenging. Without GED as an option what would happen to these students? The outcomes for students without any hope of a secondary credential are bleak. We can imagine the increase in crime rates, violence, drug use, and people on public assistance.

Instead of these negative outcomes, the GED is a step in the right direction. Students can achieve success and learn about educational and career options. But the GED is not a quick fix. Sometimes it is viewed as the easy way out. High school staff may encourage struggling students—or students who are challenging—to drop out and get a GED. This is not an advisable approach. At PCC we work with students and encourage them to stay in high school whenever possible.

A GED alone should not be the ultimate goal of any GED program. Just getting passing scores on the GED tests will do little to ensure future success in college and careers. Our job as practitioners is to provide access to the "next step" for students. We need to make sure students leave us with the 21st-century skills necessary to move forward with their lives—whether in college or a career. In our YES program we engage students in conversations about their hopes and dreams. We expose them to career options. We attempt to keep them enrolled, building their skills until they can pass their GED tests with the highest possible scores.

Everyone's Job: Contributing to Program Success

The members of our staff work as a team to understand student needs and reengage students with education. We provide individualized services to students so that each student can complete a high school or college credential and begin a career or continue his or her education. Our mission statement really captures our goal: "PCC Prep: Empowering students through personalized support, educational innovation, and academic excellence." Our staff are experts at supporting students' needs without enabling them. We model what we expect to see in students and empower them to become their best selves. We believe in getting in the way of students' failure. We practice intrusive advising and actively engage students in changing the patterns that have not helped them in the past.

Student success is everyone's job. All staff members take part in meeting the needs of students, including faculty, managers, and front office staff. Faculty spend hours tutoring and meeting individually with students. They collaborate with other staff and work together to make sure each student sees the relevance of what he or she is studying. The members of our front office staff help students navigate college systems. From helping them understand bills, to providing bus tickets and the occasional cup of coffee, they create a family environment where everyone is welcome. The managers in our office see the big picture but also focus on individual students' needs. They often drop what they are doing to answer questions or help a student in crisis. This team work ethic creates an environment of support and inclusion.

At the center of this nurturing environment are our College Success Coaches. The coach provides each student with personalized advising, case management, referrals to resources, mentoring, and tutoring. The coach is the person students go to when they are about to become homeless or when they break up with their significant other. The coach knows when a student is having a relapse or if a student needs help keeping the electricity on in his or her house. From providing a meal to going shopping with a student to pick out a prom dress, the coach is a tireless supporter and cheerleader. However, the coach also holds students accountable. Through tough love and respect, the coach keeps each student engaged and on track. This special relationship allows us to customize the educational experience for each student and provide carrots—and sticks—as necessary.

What Is the Role of the Practitioner?

GED programs exist to pick up the pieces. Individuals, systems, and circumstances have failed young people and they come to us to change their future. Our charge is a big one:

- We must focus on students' strengths and shed light on a new path for their future.
- We must have high standards and expectations while also allowing flexibility and understanding for students' circumstances.
- We must hire staff that "get it" and are passionate about this population.
- We must embrace differences and foster cultural competency in our environment and curriculum.
- We must be innovators. The needs of our students change and our practices and supports need to change with them.
- We must be advocates in our local communities, at the state level, and at the national level. If we don't speak up, voices from this marginalized population will *not* be heard.
- We must champion rigor. It is easy to want to support students by helping them too much and not insisting on high standards.
- We must find supporters and advocates in our communities and work hard to maintain those relationships. We cannot do this work in isolation and expect it to be sustainable.
- We must be on the continual search for best practices. GED programs are not properly networked and should be sharing and learning together.

What Still Needs to Be Done

This is a pivotal time in education reform. We are moving away from focusing on access and heading toward a completion agenda. This is an important shift. It makes way for the GED to be viewed as one measure of success. Although attainment of a GED is a completion, it cannot be the end goal for our students. We need citizens prepared to think critically, with a wide array of skills including solid skills in math, science, and technology. This requires post-GED plans and enrollment in workforce training or college programs.

The new GED was released test in January 2014. To pass the new test students will have to develop deeper skills and be more computer literate. With higher expectations for our students, GED programs also must change instructional strategies in order for students to succeed. At PCC we are in the midst of changing our YES GED program with some ideas gleaned from best practice GED programs around the country. We are incorporating lessons learned from the Back on Track work done by Jobs for the Future. In the past, the number of GEDs completed measured our success. Now we must show postsecondary preparedness and enrollment. We are examining the best way to make this shift and plan to launch our renamed program "YES to College" in the next year.

As champions for the GED we must change the cultural understanding of what the GED is and how important it is to access and equity in education. We need to continue to tell the stories of our students and push forward to get the GED accepted as a legitimate secondary credential. Messaging and marketing strategies created collaboratively among those of us doing this work can help this effort. We can work together to send a clear message that a GED is a tool for students to move forward with their dreams.

There is a lot of work to be done in preparing students and their families for the cultural and class shift that education brings. GED program staff can work with students to develop strategies to address this divide. Sometimes students leave their educational dreams behind when they begin to see themselves shut out by their families. Former students have described a feeling of living in two worlds when they surpass their parents' educational attainment. GED programs need to provide more engagement for families to help them understand and support their children's successes and develop courses and counseling for students to navigate this cultural shift.

We need GED champions. Although there are a few progressive foundations and educational leaders who see the value of the GED, we still do not have the critical mass necessary to make systemic change. Individuals in government along with private businesses could make a big difference by offering their support and contributing their money to promote the GED as a legitimate bridge to college and careers.

As practitioners, we are on a path to improving outcomes for GED graduates. There are many barriers and challenges, but we must continue to adapt and evolve our services to help the neediest students. At PCC, we hope to be a part of a growing national culture of GED to college models. We plan to continue to share best practices and create space for ongoing collaboration locally and nationally. Together, with other practitioners, it will be possible to support students in ways that we cannot on our own. We will not give up on our students, as others have in the past. We will continue to believe in them until they can believe in themselves.

8

INSTITUTIONAL RESPONSE
AT THE COLLEGE LEVEL

Santa Fe Scholars Program as a Model for the Future

Jackson Sasser

Education costs money, but then so does ignorance.

—Claus Moser

Santa Fe College, one of the top 10 community colleges in the country, a charter member of the League for Innovation, and a leader in educational attainment, has launched a nationally recognized program that is enhancing access, persistence, and success of General Education Development (GED®) certificate holders at the postsecondary level.

While all community colleges serve students, this new program enables students themselves to serve other students. This is a kind of force multiplier that dramatically expands the capabilities of our college staff by enlisting volunteer assistance from top students who have been specifically trained to help their peers.

It is fitting that students are given such a responsible role. "Student-centeredness" is the principle upon which Santa Fe College was founded more than 40 years ago and remains my guiding philosophy as president today. This fall Santa Fe received the distinction of being named one of the nation's top 10 community colleges by the Aspen Institute. When the news was unveiled to an audience of college, community, and state leaders, it was appropriate that I arranged to have our student body president make the historic announcement.

Students were essential in Santa Fe receiving the recognition. The Aspen Institute bases its selection of top colleges on student academic achievement, degree and college completion, minority and low-income student accomplishment, and job placement. At Santa Fe we have a long and distinguished record of student success. Our graduation rates exceed those of any college in the state of Florida. Because the college had a solid foundation in meeting high standards and exceeding expectations, we were in a good position to build upward and devote more attention to smaller and well-defined communities of students requiring additional attention. One such group is students who have a GED certificate rather than a high school diploma.

A Focus on Serving Students With GEDs

Santa Fe has a full complement of services to enable students to succeed. We offer academic advising, career counseling, personal counseling, learning labs, remedial education known as academic foundations, and adult education to boost students' academic skills in reading, writing, and mathematics. Despite these prodigious efforts, the ability to persist in college remained a problem for our GED students.

The idea for a program to address the specific needs of GED holders developed out of an alternative spring break trip open to all students through the Office of Civic Engagement and Service to Washington, DC, that the college sponsored several years ago. Students were selected based on their involvement with the college and community, as well as their desire to serve others. Dr. Angela Long, then an advisor to Santa Fe's student organizations, organized the trip, which included volunteer work at a food bank and in an elementary school. A highlight was the opportunity to meet with Under Secretary of Education Martha Kanter, the first community college leader to serve in this position. She spoke with our students about a dropout crisis in education and welcomed their suggestions to address the problem.

With guidance from Dr. Long, our students rose to the challenge. Working together, they developed a proposal for a three-year pilot program at Santa Fe designed to increase retention, persistence, and graduation rates of nontraditional GED completers seeking degrees. They selected GED holders because Dr. Long had extensively researched them for her doctoral dissertation, GED students have high dropout rates, and the problem is magnified in Florida. While 1 in 12 students enrolled in his or her first year of college nationwide is a GED holder, the ratio in Florida is 1 in 10 students. They cannot be ignored. When Dr. Long and her students proposed a program for GED holders, I extended my full support. I made provisions to allocate $10,000 from the Student Life Department for its operation, revised Dr. Long's job description to enable her to serve as the new program's director, and pledged whatever resources I could to encourage the initiative's success. The program is called the Pathways to Persistence Scholars Program because it is designed to put students on the pathway to realizing a life-sustaining career.

Pathways to Persistence Scholars Program

Appropriately enough, Pathways is based on a student leadership model. At Santa Fe, students not only lead other students, but also are actively involved in the decision-making process of the college. They serve on the president's cabinet and attend coordinating council meetings alongside the leadership of our college. They are not there simply as advisors or observers; they are an essential part of our governance structure, and their recommendations are heeded in the establishment of programs and policies.

Leadership and Service

Students are given substantial leadership responsibilities in the Pathways to Persistence program. Each incoming student is assigned a "Peer Connector," a student from within the student government, the Phi Theta Kappa honorary society, the honors program, or the college's student ambassador program. Peer Connectors meet at least once a week with Pathways to Persistence students to assist them with studying and connecting to campus resources and activities. The students are well prepared to step into an important leadership role. They are encouraged and supported. Santa Fe's culture entails the highest expectations for our students while giving them the education and training they need to succeed.

Students who benefit from Pathways are groomed to be leaders. From the beginning they are encouraged to believe they have much to offer the college, because they do. Their introduction to Pathways is a personal letter that begins by congratulating them for receiving a GED, praise they may not be accustomed to hearing or associating with having the credential. They are invited to a personal interview with the Pathways director to learn they have an opportunity to be a voice for the nation in the name of fellow GED students.

Students are motivated to succeed because they are treated as leaders. As testament to the status accorded them, participants wear gold name tags bearing the words "Pathways Scholar"; *scholar* is a term that seldom had been applied to their academic performance in the past. Incoming students, along with their families, attend an evening banquet where they are recognized as scholars and welcomed into the college environment. Other components of the program encourage students to integrate into campus life and fall in love with the college. One evening a week they take a "college success" class that offers tips, advice, and information about how to adapt to, negotiate, and persevere in the college setting. Each student is assigned a member of the faculty as a mentor, who, with his or her knowledge about the complexities of the college, is willing and able to assist in navigating the system. Academic advisement and early alert systems are in place so that professors may intervene early to stem a problem, thus enhancing student opportunities for success. By their second year in the program, students are prepared to lead. They mentor, become officers in the Persistent Scholars Club, serve on college committees, and participate in community volunteer projects.

Leadership begins, as the aphorism goes, at the top. As president, I found one of my most important responsibilities with Pathways to be selecting the right person to direct the program. Ideal candidates had to have strong leadership qualities and a passion for serving students. They had to be able to nurture and inspire them to be leaders. It is a formidable task. The students in the Pathways program are among our most disadvantaged. They face daunting challenges and operate upon some of the most fragile foundations. Some have been homeless, lived in cars, or literally not had much to eat for days. In a single year one student experienced a heart attack, foreclosure on his house, a fight for custody of his grandchild, the suicide of a relative, and the death of his father.

Overcoming the Odds

Students triumph despite the odds. One young woman who dropped out of high school after living in foster homes and being abused now takes classes at night while working as a hairdresser. Pathways led another student away from a life of crime to air force aspirations. Instead of following his friends stealing cars and breaking into houses, he listens to his mentor, our campus police chief. Another young man, who thought about ending his life, is now considering pursuing a bachelor's degree in health services administration. He is president of the Persistent Scholars Club and recruits volunteers to tutor students in the program. The strong support students receive from their peers, who themselves often experienced hardships yet persevered, is a leading reason the program succeeds for so many.

I listened to these and other students' stories for several hours at a holiday program on campus. It was one of the most inspiring evenings of my presidency. Consistently, I find that insights from students such as these allow me to serve them more effectively. I make an effort to keep those lines of communication open by attending as many student functions as possible.

I look forward to the initiation banquet for Pathways students and to other special activities in the program. I make a concerted effort to involve others. When students and Dr. Long proposed the idea for Pathways, I invited faculty, staff, and the vice president for student affairs to my office to hear their presentation.

Campuswide Involvement

A vexing problem is that useful services are often nearby yet seem remote or nonexistent to many educationally and otherwise disadvantaged students. So, involving others from various parts of campus gives many a stake in the program and its success. A wide network of faculty and staff from different departments is affiliated with and, more important, engaged in the Pathways program, which ensures the students' informed access to campus resources. An employee in financial aid who is an advisor to Pathways makes it known he is there to serve the students and understands their problems. The same holds true for other staff in counseling and various other student services and in the academic departments. The program would be much less effective without their commitment.

Community Involvement

Our readiness to involve the campus community extends to the broader community. Just as we collaborate with business and community leaders in our workforce initiatives, we do so in our academic programs and student services. A promising partnership has begun between Pathways and the Gainesville Job Corps, a career/technical training program under the U.S. Department of Labor, to help students make a smooth transition to community college. Other collaborations are in various stages of development. Working with the Rotary Club of Downtown Gainesville, Pathways students raised money for a trip to Washington, DC, to present preliminary results of the program to U.S. Department of Education officials. In addition, the Pathways program has adopted a Gainesville highway in its name while participating in area cleanups, and students have spoken to inmates at a local prison about getting a GED and the merits of the Pathways program.

In our community, Santa Fe has earned a reputation for innovation. We are a key member of a successful and new public-private initiative called Innovation Gainesville, which mustered the best of economic development and government cooperation and applied higher education to lure a multinational company and 400 high-paying jobs to the city. Innovation and a willingness to take risks also define Pathways. Because Pathways is unique, I had no precedent to follow in its establishment. I took the calculated risk of following the untested but reasoned advice of students and Dr. Long in authorizing the program and securing funds to finance it. Just as seed money fosters the growth of start-up companies, a small investment can pay huge dividends in student development. I also encourage innovation across the college. I do not deter others at the college from taking risks, especially ones wisely taken. There is much to be gained from the cost-effective wager. At its worst there is a small loss, but the people of the college feel assured that they are welcome to try. At its best there are national high-caliber programs like Pathways. When our employees succeed, so do our college and community. Accordingly, their achievements must be praised, nurtured, and sustained.

Pay It Forward

Providing rewards for good work fosters pride, confidence, and a resulting sense of duty to give back and serve others. I call it "pay it forward." This attitude is apparent in the Pathways program and throughout our college. One of our counselors, who emigrated from another country, was inspired to become a Pathways advisor by the tremendous support she encountered as a newcomer at Santa Fe. Likewise, Pathways students, who thrive from the personal attention they receive during their first year, give back their second year by orienting the next group of students in the program. "Pay it forward" can now be seen at the national level. Pathways students traveled to Washington, DC, in spring 2012 to present preliminary results of the program to White House officials. Their achievements and the lessons they learned will spread to others as Pathways is considered for national duplication.

Final Thoughts: The Role of Administration

The role of college leadership will be essential in developing and promoting services and programs that retain GED students. Advancement of the community college core missions of access, opportunity, and success is accomplished by the following recommendations in developing initiatives and programs for students with GEDs:

- Welcome and encourage suggestions from students. There is no better way to develop innovative and creative ideas than by gathering a range of student perspectives, from those of student government leaders to those of students who have considered dropping out or have actually left school.
- Involve staff and students in decision making and the design of retention programs.
- Take calculated risks in dedicating funds to a program that can pay large dividends in student retention.

- Foster a college climate that promotes trust, innovation, and acceptance of diverse ideas. All benefit by rewarding good work and encouraging a sense of duty to give back and serve others.
- Provide the resources and tools to administrators that make it possible for them to design successful programs.
- Involve the community and individual departments on campus so that everyone has a stake. Such efforts should include allowing family members of the students to attend special events along with inviting community leaders so they can learn firsthand about and see the value of the program on and off campus.
- Throughout the school promote a "pay it forward" attitude, in which beneficiaries of good deeds repay others.

We at Santa Fe celebrate our students' accomplishments and look forward to being part of a growing national conversation that holds such promise in transforming educational opportunities for generations to come.

PART THREE

THE VOICE OF THE STUDENT: PROMOTING RETENTION FROM A STUDENT LEADERSHIP PERSPECTIVE

9

FROM GED® TO MASTER'S DEGREE

Leah Rapoza

The beautiful thing about learning is that no one can take it away from you.

—B. B. King

They say that a picture is worth a thousand words. The photo on the following page (Figure 9.1) is of the house my family was living in when I was born. I suppose I am using the term *house* loosely—really it was an old army tent. It was one of the many interesting places my mom, my dad, my three sisters, my brother, and I would live in as part of our childhood. By the time I was 10, I could count 26 "houses" that we had occupied.

I was born in Hilo, Hawai'i, and lived there for nine months, at which point my family relocated to Oregon. We lived in Portland for a while and then moved around Central Oregon more times than I can count. When I was five we moved to Michigan for six months and lived with my grandparents. Though I have a few memories from before then, only the memories from that point on are truly clear. I remember that in Michigan I started kindergarten and I *loved* it. That was my first taste of formal education.

We moved back to Central Oregon over winter break, and though I was put into a new kindergarten where we were living in Madras, I attended only a few weeks before being pulled out of school. My mother was working a few jobs to make ends meet and picking me up became too difficult. Sadly my public school career ended because I was left at school one too many times. From that day forward, I was homeschooled by my older sisters.

Figure 9.1 The family "house."

At the age of seven I moved back to Hawai'i with my family. As I recall, I loved most of my time while there. My paternal grandparents lived close by and I quickly grew attached to them. All of the homes in which I lived in Hawai'i lent themselves to great adventures. One house was on 300 acres of rain forest. Imagine all the fun five children could have with 300 acres to explore. The only house I didn't like had the most awful shower imaginable. It still makes me cold thinking about it. There was a 10-foot-by-10-foot cement room in the basement with a showerhead and only cold water. Needless to say, bath time was not a favorite pastime of mine.

When I was 10, we moved back to Portland. My mom started working a few jobs, as usual, and a few of her coworkers needed babysitters while they were at work. This started a new phase of my life. I was immediately hired, and the children in the first group that I babysat were each a struggle for me to handle; I was just a little girl myself, but I quickly learned tips and tricks to manage them. By the end of that year, I was babysitting 40 hours a week while supporting myself and my family as best as I could. This pretty much ended my homeschooling. But despite the loss of learning, I loved watching the kids. I would take them on walks, have them do crafts, and teach them things. There were times I wished so much that I could have a life like a normal preteen, but for the most part I avoided thinking about it. In the end, it all worked out. After all, these years were the beginning of my professional development as a teacher.

When I was 16, my mom wanted me to officially drop out from the homeschool experience, which led me to pursue my General Education

Development (GED®) certificate. To this day, I believe that my mother felt it was time for me to move on with my life and start working more. A GED was the next logical step toward adulthood. I learned of a program at Portland Community College that promised to help me prepare for the GED test. It was quite a daunting experience because I had never written a paper before or done more than basic mathematics. Needless to say, I had more than a little catch-up work to do.

Something amazing happened in that program, however—I found that I *loved* to learn. I loved everything about school; I loved having teachers, I loved getting to learn new things, and I even loved homework. The teachers in the YES (Youth Empowered to Succeed) GED program recognized my passion for learning and encouraged me to pursue my diploma in a high school completion program after I completed my GED. The high school completion program I entered, Gateway to College, offered the opportunity for me to earn both high school and college credits at the same time. (Interestingly, Oregon is one of the only states to allow a person to earn both a GED and a high school diploma.)

I had never before in my life considered going to college. Yet, by chance I was given an opportunity to enter the world of education. I loved having teachers, learning new things, and the idea of gaining exposure to opportunities was extremely appealing. Starting the program meant getting up by 5:00 a.m., taking a two-hour bus ride to school, and transferring three times while en route. I recall many cold, dark mornings, but I knew that school was waiting on the other side and that made it worth it. After a long day of school, I would wait for a different bus and then head to work for the remainder of the day. As I look back now, I can honestly say that I learned so much while in the program and gained so many amazing role models whom I continue to count on to this day.

Within two weeks of enrollment, it was confirmed in my heart that I wanted to become a teacher. More important, I was already planning my next steps toward the right college or university to attend, as well as the necessary strides to get there. I spent the next four years working diligently to catch up on everything I had missed learning in my younger years. Eventually, I completed the program and graduated with my high school diploma. I will never forget the moment I held that degree in my hand, knowing that it was my ticket to entrance and transfer into any college of my choice.

From Student to Teacher

Upon graduating from Portland Community College, I immediately enrolled at Portland State University. An opportunity arose for me to live on campus, so I moved into the dorms and lived among other students. This was a new world for me and I was able to taste all of the traditional experiences that other students had been given. I loved having the library right there, being surrounded by people learning all the time, and feeling like a part of the school community. Within two years, I earned my BA in social science with a minor in elementary education and immediately transferred into PCC's graduate education program with a focus on teacher licensure.

The graduate program experience proved to be some of the best years of my life. For the first time since I had started school, I was able to tell people my story and truly be myself. I had always worried that people would look down on me. I still do worry about people looking down on me every time I share my story; however, I found that my peers not only accepted my background, but came to respect it. In the teaching world, it has allowed me to recognize a perspective that many students have come from, but one that not many teachers understand.

Less than one year ago, I made a firm decision to go back to school to earn a second master's degree, in special education. I take classes at night while working and living near an elementary school that has a 78% poverty rate. It is ingrained in my heart to be surrounded by students who are struggling with issues similar to those I did while growing up. I am able to tell them that things can get better, and when they know my story they can actually believe it.

Many Chances to Give Up

Despite the many amazing moments in my journey through education, there have been equally devastating moments where I almost gave up entirely. For example, when I walked into my first GED class, I was 16 and had not been in a school environment for more than 10 years. I had no idea what I was getting myself into when I stepped onto campus that day. I quickly learned just how much I didn't know. Even my peers in the program were so much more advanced than I was. I had never written a paper; I didn't even know where to begin. Those of you in higher education know just how important writing is in order to be successful. Yet, I didn't know the importance of writing for me, and furthermore, I felt I couldn't do it. I didn't know how to sit at a desk, let alone raise my hand to answer a question. And on that first day, I felt like I was in a world where I did not belong. *This* was the first moment that I truly considered giving up.

When I finished the YES GED program, the instructors suggested I continue my education. I was very excited about the idea and was ready to start right away. My mother did not want me to continue because she said it would interrupt my work schedule and felt it was better that I focused solely on work. Her lack of encouragement was devastating. At that point, I realized there would be no support from my family, and thereafter I delayed enrollment for an entire term as I once again considered dropping out.

Getting through the first term of school was very hard. There were many mornings when my alarm would go off and I would have to fight the temptation to stay at home and forget it all. Without the support of my family, I was responsible for getting to the school, completing all my homework, and balancing a job. As I look back on my life now, with many terms of graduate school completed, I can see that that first term was the hardest of my educational life.

It is important to note that colleges lose many students during the first term due to the often incredibly difficult transition with no support. The temptation to give up was a daily battle for me despite the fact that I was learning new and exciting things. I had a deep desire to share my experiences with the family I loved, but they expressed no interest in what I was doing and learning.

As the classes became more difficult, the lack of family support worsened. I was working a lot, and when I arrived home each evening to do homework, there was no place for me to do it. School was seen as something that interfered with my ability to work and help around the house, so a place to study was not going to be provided. I spent many hours crying while curled up on the bathroom floor with my homework in hand. It turned out the bathroom was the only quiet place in the entire house where I could focus on my studies.

A key moment in my life occurred when I realized that despite my efforts in wanting my family to care about my schooling it was never going to happen. It was then and there that I made the decision that I needed to move out and get my own apartment with a friend if I was to continue being successful. This was one of the hardest decisions I ever made. My family did not want me to move out, and therefore, we didn't speak for months. Even though I had to travel farther to get to school and I had more financial burdens, I had a place where I could study and the constant negativity from my family about school was gone. In retrospect, I realize I could have easily given up then as well, but I did not.

After some time, my relationship with my family improved a bit, but there were still moments when their words cut me like a knife. I remember the day I received my acceptance letter to graduate school. It was a fairly competitive program and I was so excited to have received word I would be able to attend. I was proud and I wanted to share my excitement. I went to my parents' house and ran in the door, unable to contain my exhilaration. I told my mom that I had gotten into the education program; I was going to become a teacher! I will never forget her words or the look in her eyes. She said, "Why do you continue to waste your life? Why can't you do something worthwhile with your life and have babies, like your sister?!" I realized at that moment I would never be accepted by my family. I no longer belonged. And at that moment, for the first time, I not only considered quitting but wished that I had never gone to school.

The memories I have described are not the most encouraging, yet they are so important and critical to the issue of GED graduates pursuing higher education. Many students with GEDs experience challenges similar to the ones I did; I am not an anomaly. These challenges (or ones similar) are likely the reason that many students with GEDs drop out of school. It is not an easy road; it is one where we have to fight every day of our lives to get through. It is exhausting, which makes it very easy to just give up. It is important for all of us to figure out how to help students become more successful and to answer the questions, Why don't students give up when the challenges get hard? and What supports help them continue?

The Support of Strangers

To answer the first of the two questions just posed, I am able to sum up the reason why I did not give up as easily as I could have: I found the support of strangers. When I entered the YES GED program 10 years ago, I was completely unprepared for the experience. The professors I had during my first term took an interest in me and in my education. I had two instructors in particular who were willing to help me in any way they could. They cared about me and opened up their hearts. I had never had anyone care about my education before. These two women told me I was smart and could learn. They held high standards and did not accept excuses. Despite the struggles, I wanted to make them proud and worked day and night to gain the skills I needed to do so. It was because of these instructors who reached out to me during my early stages of education that I was able to acquire the much-needed support to get through.

While battling my mother's disappointment over me pursuing my education, as opposed to working full-time and "settling down," I struggled with rejection and the desire to earn her approval. I was very fortunate to come into contact with an amazing professor at Portland State University during that time who offered me support. She had come from a background of poverty as well and had shared this with our class the last day of the term. In my attempt to be understood, I wrote her a letter and asked if we could meet. She agreed, and over a cup of coffee she told me her story and allowed me to share mine. Practically a complete stranger, she connected with me and told me she was proud of me! Her words of validation confirmed that this process in life would be painful but that my feelings were legitimate and someday it would get better. Despite "disappointing" my family, I knew others who were proud of the things I had accomplished. This changed my life and prompted me to work as hard as I possibly could.

The day I announced my acceptance to graduate school to my mother and was asked why I couldn't do something meaningful with my life was one of the hardest days of my life. I remember returning that night to my dorm, collapsing on the floor, and shaking with sobs for hours. I believe this was the moment I realized the world I came from would never truly accept me and I would never truly belong again. I belonged to no one and fit nowhere. After calming myself down, I proceeded to e-mail a woman whom I had met previously at a conference. She had been incredibly supportive of me at the time and I respected her opinion greatly. My e-mail expressed many things including the fact that I did not belong anywhere and didn't know what to do.

Not long after, I received a reply from this mentor. She consoled me and brought up a point that I had not considered in my blind state of fear and pain: I did not fit in either world anymore. I was neither fish nor fowl. This did, however, put me in a unique place to help others. I still struggle with the issue of not belonging, but her words helped me to see that despite the great challenges that came with my situation, I also have a unique opportunity to help people in a way that others cannot. In that very moment, I knew I could not give up, no matter how hard it would be for me. I determined I was going to make it through.

Often I am asked if I am resentful toward my family. There have been moments of resentment, but I genuinely know in my heart that it is not their fault. I don't believe my mother ever meant to hurt me. She simply didn't understand my need for an education, and often people fear things they do not understand. In reality, she worked very hard to provide for her family, and from her vantage point, school was expensive and perhaps a huge waste of money. Her culture and my belief systems did not align, which I eventually learned to accept.

Understanding the Whole Story

My experiences are also the experiences of countless others. Students like me come from poverty, as well as from broken homes, both literally and figuratively. We know that we must eat everything on our plate because we never know when we will eat again. We know that extra blankets work when the heat does not. We are told our whole lives we are not smart enough, not good enough, and we will fail. We know that life isn't fair. But, despite all of that, we come, we enter college, and we *try* to change our lives.

Education is supposed to be the great equalizer. America is supposed to be the country where if you are willing to work hard enough you can pull yourself up. The truth is, however, that our education system is designed to set up students who are from diverse backgrounds to fail. And fail they do. Students who live in poverty and those who do not finish high school or those who receive GEDs fail out of college every day. Most of those who fail do so before they finish their first term.

You may ask, "Why do so many students with GEDs drop out of college? Why do students from these backgrounds drop out so early?" Some say it is because "those people" are lazy. "They" don't work hard enough. But consider this: If that were the truth, why would they sign up for college in the first place? Students from diverse backgrounds enter college because they want to work hard. They want to change their lives. They try, and yes, sadly, many times they fail. But, in my opinion, it is not of their own accord but, rather, because of a system that is not designed to support them.

Students who are entering college face many barriers, specifically the lack of a working knowledge of a school environment. For many, college was never discussed at home. To a student who grew up in an affluent household with two parents who attended college, entering the college world is a natural process and the student has family to go to in the event that he or she does not understand something. To a student with a GED who has never known anyone who went to college, entering the college world is like moving to a foreign country. Everyone speaks a different language than the student. The average three-year-old in a family with high socioeconomic status knows more words than an adult living in poverty.

Another big challenge for many students is the lack of family support. This is a particularly difficult one. For families living in poverty, the social support of the family unit is huge. Families face obstacles every day—hunger, pain, homelessness—but the one thing that they can count on is each other. Ideally, families from all walks of life get along and spend time with each other. But in homes struggling with poverty, family may be the only driving force. It is a huge part of what makes these individuals strong. A strong family unit can therefore be a problem for students from lower socioeconomic status families who are entering college. Students may leave school to go back and take care of the family. When family support is such a big deal, education often takes a back burner. Personally, I know that a large number of students drop out because of family-related issues.

Families may also see education as a threat to the home unit itself. Often family members will feel intimidated when another member is pursuing an education. It is almost as if a message is being sent by the student that his or her home life is not good enough. As a result, this can be very hurtful to the individual members of the home because they may conclude that the student believes himself or herself to be "better" than anyone else. Therefore, education becomes a negative experience, and family members often force students to choose between family and school. This is a major reason why we lose many students.

Consider first that students often grow up seeing the family unit as the only source of strength. It is almost as if students are then asked to choose between losing education and losing the only world they know: their family support structure. Such a decision would be hard for anyone to make. In reality, some students *do* choose education and, as a result, lose family support.

Late in my undergrad years, I took a consumer health class. One particular evening, the class discussion revolved around the concept of society being set up to improve people's lives through education. I asked, "Is it truly improving people's lives if we educate them only for them to be rejected by the only support system they know?" Needless to say, no one gave an adequate response to my question. It was at this point in my life that I realized I did not belong anymore. I was angry. How could the system have done this to me? How could it knowingly turn me into something that was accepted nowhere? How could this improve my life?

While having coffee with a professor willing to talk the situation out, I began to come to the conclusion that the system is broken. But it isn't broken in the sense that we shouldn't be admitting students to college. It is broken in the sense that we are not providing the support structure to students that they need in order to be successful once they transition to college. Consider this: You cannot take a person out of an environment and put that person into a strange one, take away that person's support network, and then expect that person to be successful. I am a teacher. I know in education this will not work. Essentially, we are setting students up to fail. Need proof? Fifty percent of students drop out of school. It isn't just a few students falling through the cracks. We are setting up 50% of our workforce for failure and telling a lie about America being a country where you can do anything if you work hard enough.

The good news is, we don't have to! We can support these students, and truthfully it won't take very much. We have a broken system but it is one that could be easily adapted. What do students need in order to be successful? The answer is pretty simple.

Support, Support, Support

Support. Students need support. They need peer support and support of people in higher education. They need to know that when they do not understand something they have someone to whom they can go and ask. They need to know that when their family is telling them they are worthless, they can go to someone who will tell them they are smart. They need to know that they are not alone. Here are some suggestions as to how this can be done:

- Provide support staff assigned to specific students for counseling and guidance.
- Offer peer tutoring and a peer buddy system (i.e., mentorship from those who have gone on from getting their GED to college).
- Encourage a social support network (a sort of replacement family) for those who are not getting their support elsewhere.
- Offer study skills classes.
- Provide for families resources that give information on college, its culture, and so on.

I am where I am today because of strangers. I am here because strangers reached out to me and were there to hug me when I felt dejected. They were there to share my accomplishments. They were there to answer my questions about school. They didn't laugh at me when I didn't know something. I am here because along the way people offered me the one thing that is the difference between success and failure: support.

10

THE POWER OF STUDENT LEADERSHIP IN TRANSFORMING LIVES

Frederick Parks Jr.

Wisdom is not the product of schooling, but the lifelong attempt to acquire it.

—Albert Einstein

A gentleman stood in front of a class of students one day and held up a twenty-dollar bill. He asked the class, "Who would like to have this twenty-dollar bill?" Everyone immediately raised their hand. After a few moments, he threw the bill down to the floor and stepped on it. "Now, who would still like this twenty-dollar bill?" Everyone's hand was still raised. Next, the gentleman crumpled the bill into a ball and proceeded to ask his usual question. Everyone's hand still stood high. Finally, the gentleman chose to rip the bill in half. "Now, who would still like this twenty-dollar bill?" All of the students still chose to raise their hand with utmost fervor. "That's amazing," said the gentleman. "It never fails that whenever I do a public speaking engagement and ask this question, not a single hand goes down. However, whenever I apply these same contexts to people, I never get quite the same response." The students looked at him with puzzled faces. "Every day, students come to school from all walks of life and we never know their pasts or where they've been, just like this bill. But, unlike this bill, whenever students come to us battered, broken, or torn apart emotionally, we never choose to fully accept them. Therefore, we must simply be saying that a human being's life is far less valuable than this mere twenty-dollar bill." The room was silent.

I was that gentleman speaking before a group of students at a leadership conference. But I am also that twenty-dollar bill. Growing up, I experienced many forms of pain. My family endured the severest of poverty, all the way to the point of hunger and homelessness. I have experienced emotional pain from the separation of my parents at a very young age coupled with a long separation from any father figures in my life. I have also experienced the pain of seeing others who never lacked a thing flourish before my eyes while I watched my siblings attempt to excel academically and socially on empty stomachs. I was that twenty-dollar bill, crumpled, torn apart, and stepped on without anyone acknowledging my present value. But, thankfully, through my mother's persevering love and hard work we made ends meet and continued to don the garment of success. However, without the investment of very particular academic instructors, I would never be where or what I am today. There were a handful of teachers and professors who saw my potential and truly believed in me, leading me to want to "pay it forward" and invest that same patience, love, and kindness in future generations of students, which was why I decided to help cofound the Pathways to Persistence Scholars Program and become the student leader I am today.

My mother and father were two amazing parents. After conceiving my eldest sister at a young age, my mother dropped out of school. She later obtained her General Education Development (GED®) certificate so that she could properly raise her first child, thus deciding it was best for my father to complete his high school education instead. However, after 12 years of marriage, my mother and father decided to divorce. Although my mother worked hard to complete a technical degree, it was exceptionally difficult being raised by a single mother with limited education. We faced many struggles together, sometimes to the point of extreme poverty. I remember one night for dinner the only thing that we could afford was a burger from the dollar menu of McDonald's. So we split it in four pieces, one for each of my siblings and me, and my mother went to bed hungry.

Through all of these trials, my mother taught me that the greatest asset any man would ever have was faith, not money. So I continued to read scripture and gravitate toward the positive influences in my life, such as my middle school Future Farmers of America (FFA) advisor. Because of his diligence, I was able to persist and became a statewide FFA champion. I became engrossed with the concept of a "purpose-driven life," even before the bestselling novel *The Purpose-Driven Life* was published. I read positive books to figure out why I was placed on this earth and the reason for my family's daily suffering, and why no one would help us. The only thing that continued to permeate and uplift my soul was my inner voice, daily fortified by this process. I felt like a burning coal daily pushed through a furnace, my suffering fortifying me into something amazing.

Over time, I came to believe that the reason for our trials was for this very process to take place. I assumed an attitude of grandeur believing that my creator allowed these things to happen to me to build character and to do something amazing for others in my position who were not as character driven or self-motivated. I was meant to help people! Without experiencing the bittersweet taste of tribulation, I would never know or appreciate the daily circumstances that billions of people continuously endure, and how difficult it is to simply "rise" out of those situations like we are so simply instructed to do in the media. Now, I know that like so many leaders before me, it is my spiritual and social obligation to be a shining light for the paths of others. Using the "10,000 hours" concept of practicing, studying, and learning every day, I actively and proactively work to accomplish my goals.

As the third of four children consisting of two older sisters and one younger brother, I was blessed with a guide to know that college was an option for me. As a result of my eldest sister's continual hard work and dedication, I knew that I had to go to college. Because of my high school academy, I knew that I wanted to take my agricultural biotechnology experiences and work in the areas of medical research, but I needed more time to figure out that path. So, I decided to attend a community college, which was probably one of the wisest decisions I had ever made.

My Contributions and Growth as a Student Leader

After starting college, I immediately began working full-time in order to make ends meet for myself. My experiences at this point in my life allowed me to stop looking at myself as a victim, but to see how victimized other students were around me. For example, working in financial aid in a work-study position revealed to me that counselors sometimes became too tired to show kindness to every single student who complained. Not only that, but some students were either ignorant about or intimidated by the financial aid process, including filling out the Free Application for Federal Student Aid (FAFSA). As I recall, students would wait in line for hours only to learn that they had to come back the next day, and some would become completely discouraged by the process and simply choose to drop out completely.

For some reason, students just seemed to naturally gravitate toward me with their concerns. Sometimes they would just voice their complaints, assuming that I could do something about it. Sometimes they would just cry. As a student, I rode my bike 10 miles to and from school three mornings a week. My personal issues combined with the lamentations of others encouraged me to officially become a student leader. I decided to join Student Government as the director of external affairs. My years of public speaking and becoming a certified Parliamentarian prepared me to speak out on legislative issues affecting our student body on a local, state, and community level.

After effectively lobbying for increased public transportation at the state level, I was invited to join the Pathways to Persistence Scholars initiative. This program was geared directly to students who were just like me: misunderstood, at risk, and less fortunate. I knew I had to jump on board. The best part about all the data obtained from the program was that it didn't only have to apply to students with a GED, but could be applied to a wide range of students from various backgrounds. I also knew that I had won the ears of my professors and administrators through my performances as a speaker. I could finally credibly speak to our administration as a student leader with advice and recommendations to help our student community at large.

Because of my background experiences and belief in the power of student voice, I was immediately intrigued when approached to help develop a program of support for GED students on my campus. Given the opportunity to cofound a brand-new program from a student leadership perspective, I was able to do a wide range of public speaking, teaching, surveying, and data collection. The concept that students are the greatest asset to our schools and to our communities was cemented in my heart. Speaking to students with their GEDs showed me that there were other students out there just like me— students who grew up with a poor hand of cards given to them in the game of life and because of their circumstances were never given a fair chance. Just like myself, they had to work full-time jobs, were discriminated against because of certain financial luxuries that they weren't afforded, and had to constantly fight just to wake up because they knew that every step that anyone else took was going to cost them 10 times the effort. I was finally able to help people who were just like I was before I could accept my value.

Through my involvement as a member of Student Government and program cofounder, I was able to experience the stories of many students who were daily slipping through the cracks of an exhausted, half-functioning educational system. However, I also witnessed other students like me who were willing to be an active voice to the nation and rise up to help others in similar circumstances. It was amazing to see the combined efforts of student leaders in Student Government and other organizations working hand in hand with selfless professors and dedicated administrators. The secret to our success was nothing less than the committed performances of all these amazing people.

Along with the main program designer, Dr. Angela Long, and two other student leaders (Austin Brinza, student body president, and Patrick McConn, student government director of external affairs), we were able to develop a program of action that soon came to be known as the Pathways to Persistence Scholars Program. The structure of the program was developed with the intent of treating GED students as scholars and welcomed family members.

When first being invited to join the Pathways program, we made sure that our students felt as though they had a sense of belonging. My experiences in FFA taught me that students respond best when they feel that they are being rewarded or honored. In other words, this wasn't a program for social rejects. We were bestowing upon them the opportunity to join something great. We did this by meeting them face-to-face from the beginning to remove any stigma of inadequacy. However, we also validated the program by putting them through an interview process. I personally felt validated in working with these fellow students by being able to share my stories with them and continually showing them that anything is possible when you believe in yourself.

Next, we made sure that our students felt involved on campus. My time as a student at Santa Fe College, the University of Florida, high school, and middle school taught me that we as students feel most appreciated and understood when we take active roles in leadership on our campuses. Our students were encouraged to join the Honors Society, Phi Theta Kappa, and Student Government. We showed them that their opinions mattered. Their past didn't have to inhibit their future unless they allowed it to take a strong-hold on their lives. Our students would also go on to lead the next cohort of students from previous semesters. These opportunities also taught them to balance their work, school, home, and personal lives with any extracurricular activities. Without student involvement, students cannot visualize their own successes. In this regard, we actively listened to their opinions and encouraged them to discover possible solutions.

Another major tenet of the Pathways program is to teach the students how to properly interact with administrators. Unfortunately, because so many of us have been stigmatized as failures, incapable, or doomed to fail, we inherit mistrust for administrators who have the power to change these stigmas. This bitterness only appears to be exacerbated by faculty who don't take a personal stake in the lives of their students and aren't afraid to call a student's mistake "stupid" in front of a class of peers. These actions leave scars in the minds of our students that take years to heal. Thankfully, there are many administrators and faculty who fully appreciate our students and proactively work to meet with them weekly. They help to organize agendas and calendars leading to graduation, listen to the students' concerns, and extend an ear of guidance and counsel. I had that going through school and it made all the difference for me. Just knowing that there were people whom I considered brilliant and willing to believe in me suggested that maybe I was brilliant too—especially if I was distinctive enough to be noticed by them.

Over my time as a student another really important concept that developed was the concept of fun. Students gravitate toward activities that are pleasurable for them. As part of the Pathways program, we made sure that our students had fun together by hosting during- and after-school activities, such as free pizza get-togethers and socials where they could relax and get to know each other. This proved imperative to building an atmosphere of camaraderie, reliability, and trust. It soon became easy for our students to meet one another outside of class to study together, relinquish their greatest fears together, and call on each other for help.

Ultimately, I believe that the greatest support for our students came from the financial aid office's assistance throughout the program. After working in the office only a few years before, I became vastly aware of the financial concerns that plagued other students, just as they had for me. Many of our students weren't knowledgeable about the process because of a lack of assistance. As with everything else, we depended on a few individuals who were self-sacrificing enough to see the needs of these students and come to their rescue.

Our advisors began to host seminars for our students to attend in order to become more knowledgeable about the FAFSA process. They were instructed on the importance of timely application, as well as actively staying in contact with an assigned advisor in order to keep up to date with any changes in the financial aid system. Students began to apply for scholarships and student loans that previously they would not have known about. This was definitely the greatest asset of the program because now these students could afford to be in school without worrying about whether their power would be shut off at home while they were studying or whether their children would go hungry. Normally, this continued cycle of fear kept our students from focusing properly at school, only guaranteeing their failure. But, through a solidified support network of amazing financial aid advisors and faculty, they were able to leave that vicious cycle and persist.

Role of the Student in Finding Motivation, Leadership, and Success

Martin Luther King Jr. once said, "The function of education is to teach one to think intensively and to think critically. Intelligence plus character—that is the goal of true education." I believe that this quote highlights the role of the student in finding motivation, leadership, and success. Surely, these are all of the qualities that a student must personally embark on a mission to acquire, but I don't believe that a traditional route will always lead to their acquisition.

In the end, life will throw all sorts of anomalies at our students. Although we'd like to think that all of our students' lives are as clear-cut as their course schedules, the majority of them are not. So, should it be said that those students who fall through the cracks merely weren't meant to be in school in the first place? Should they resign to being technical workers and laborers? I think not. I could easily have been such a student, but I chose to be the anomaly.

Student leadership is an incredibly important component of promoting retention in any college or university. It is always such an interesting paradigm whenever I attend meetings with professors, program consultants, and administrators coming together to discuss improvements for educational plans. As I glance around these rooms, I notice that I am generally the only student! This may not make sense to many, but the question that boggles my mind is, How can you know what's best for students without actually talking to them? Of course, my intention is not to offend anyone. It goes without saying that educators and faculty administrators have their degrees in education, making them the most qualified experts on educational matters. However, aren't the lesson plans and courses that these same educators went through merely making them masters and doctors of how to deal with students? So, it seems only intuitive to me that the next best thing would be to somehow directly consult various teams of students regarding educational matters in order to have direct input. Thankfully, most of the educators whom I have known are more than excited to receive student input on many matters and are always delighted when students voice their opinions in well-defined and articulate ways.

The only way to effectively cement students' desire to attend college is to allow them to have permanent roles of authority on campus where they can look back and feel as if they have contributed to the foundation of the school. Some schools have special awards and plaques for their all-star leaders, and these accomplishments are mounted on the Student Government walls for all to see. This is a great way for students who are able to be at the top of their class to feel initiated and celebrated. When students are granted opportunities for engagement with as many incentives as possible, we give them the chance to climb the ladder toward their dreams of becoming doctors, managers, and other types of professionals. The goal should therefore be to highlight their weaknesses while maximizing their strengths in order to get them to the workplace faster and not linger in school. Student leadership opportunities are a premier mechanism to allow this amazing phenomenon to occur.

How Do We Transform Education?

At the end of the day, there are many things that need to be done in order to optimize the educational system. It could be said that there isn't enough funding, but with the proper appropriation, we can do wonders with what we currently possess. It could be said that we need more officials who should care less about political agendas and more about the state of education, but without opposing views sometimes, stimulation is limited.

We must continue to remove negative stigmas and stereotypes. Each of us desires a happy existence and an optimal future, but not everyone has been dealt the same deck of cards physically, emotionally, or environmentally. By removing these stereotypes, we will allow every individual to have a chance to fail (which will undoubtedly happen one way or another) with the freedom to get back up again. History is full of second-chance heroes. But for some reason in education, these heroes aren't talked about too frequently. There isn't a basketball court you can visit during practice season that wouldn't mention an NBA professional who has fallen a few times but kicked aside his pain to keep working toward a championship trophy. The state of education is far more important than a championship win, so why aren't we as encouraging? It's time for a change.

Once our perceptions change, our realities will follow. These realities currently include our on-campus facilities where students with anything less than a perfect past have to face inward humility and shame in order to get help from anyone. If we made our financial aid process more forgiving, for example, then students who have had a bad semester and failed a course wouldn't have to spend the semester appealing, which then puts them below the required hours for financial aid. In turn, this forces them to drop out of school so they can work to bring back up their financial aid completion percentage in order to finally obtain financial aid again. It is a vicious cycle. But who is really losing out? The students who make these mistakes are mostly from single-parent homes and broken environments that don't cultivate learning. Making it difficult for those who struggle to stay in school will only continue to stimulate low socioeconomic communities, contribute to drug-related incidences, and promote poverty. Eventually, we all lose. We cannot compete globally on a national scale when our infrastructure is so broken and when we don't have educational stimulation. Education is our greatest asset.

To conclude, William Butler Yeats once said, "Education is not the filling of a pail, but the lighting of a fire." It is my hope that, if nothing else, the collective work of students such as myself, educators, administrators, and all who fight for educational reform will be able to light the greater fire for the good of humanity to be carried forward from generation to generation. It is through this flame that social change, technological advancement, and future innovation will come about, rise, and flourish in the face of an ever-changing world.

Reference

William Butler Yeats (2013). In *SearchQuotes*. Retrieved from http://www.searchquotes .com/William_Butler_Yeats/Education/quotes/.

II

REFLECTIONS OF A PEER MENTOR LEADER

Catlin Cade

Genius without education is like silver in the mine.

—Benjamin Franklin

As a first-generation college student, I have experienced many challenging adversities. Specifically, I recall May 2003. My mother, brother, and I packed our belongings and prepared for yet another move. This move was difficult for us because it followed the divorce of my mother and stepfather, who was the provider of the family. Intensifying the stress, our now single, unemployed mother of two could not find an affordable property or home. With no family living nearby, another family we knew kindly opened up their home to us. We lived with them for nine months and experienced holidays, such as Christmas and New Year's Eve, together.

Approximately one year later, after we had settled into the mobile home on property our grandfather purchased for us, my mother started a night shift job. On the days she worked, I would spend the night at our neighbor's house. On one particular night, I promised myself that I would one day earn a college degree. I made this commitment because I felt it would protect my future children from the financial struggles my family had experienced and give me the opportunity to make a greater difference in the lives of others.

Without the generosity of my grandfather, other family members, and friends, in addition to the help of government assistance, I would not be where I am today. In total, my family and I have endured two divorces and six moves. During these financial hardships, we relied on food stamps, free lunch at school, Medicaid, inconsistent child support payments, and the support of others to sustain our health and general well-being. We struggled, but I realize the situation could have been much worse without the help we received.

Support Is Fundamental

Many people crossed my path to motivate my success and prevent my failure. The actions and words of the people in my family, community, school, and church helped me to realize that I was more—more than the circumstances, more than the adversities, and more than the statistics and stereotypes that told me I could not succeed. The encouragers in my life were an ever-present reminder of the hope I had waiting for me on the other side—over the mountain of financial and situational instability—where my hard work and motivation would be evident with a college degree. Through others, I found within myself the ability to rise above my challenges.

Once I recognized that there was hope for my life, my family, and my future, I fought hard for every grade and achievement I received. I applied for additional scholarships, volunteered, took leadership roles, and did everything I could to meet the high expectations and admirations bestowed upon me. After years of resilience, I am now proud to call myself a Florida Gator. I am currently a junior and first-generation student at the University of Florida, one year away from receiving my bachelor's degree in elementary education and two years away from a master's degree in special education.

According to Spotlight on Poverty and Opportunity (2013), only 25% of low-income students complete college. Already having earned an associate of arts degree from Santa Fe College and currently pursuing a degree from the University of Florida, I feel as though I am eliminating the truth of this statistic from my life. I want many others to be able to experience the joy in overcoming the odds set against them as low-income and at-risk populations. That is why I jumped on the opportunity to become involved in the Pathways to Persistence Scholars Program for students who have earned a General Education Development (GED®) certificate and give back as I was given to by other mentors in my life.

The Power of Peer Mentoring

In August 2011, at the outset of the newly developed Pathways to Persistence Scholars Program for students with GEDs, I was approached and told of this idea for other at-risk students. The concept spoke to my heart, and after pondering the opportunity, I was asked to serve as the Peer Connector Coordinator for the program. Given full leadership authority as the student coordinator, I participated in recruiting, interviewing, and evaluating other Peer Connectors. Each Peer Connector was matched with one or two GED students and was required to contact them at least once a week. Additional requirements involved tutoring, goal setting, participating in social functions, and encouraging the students to get involved on campus. The main purpose of the Peer Connectors was to provide the GED students with a go-to person who would motivate their success, praise their achievements, and coach them through difficult times.

The role that I took in formulating the design and structure of the Peer Connector program was quite empowering. On campus, my main goal was to promote the program and the many benefits obtained at the point of involvement. Along with other student leaders, we were able to brainstorm ways to use volunteer hours for students to give back through tutoring, social support, and mentoring. As a student group, we determined that in order to become a Peer Connector, a student must have leadership experience, through involvement in either Phi Theta Kappa, student government, the Ambassadors Program, the National Honor Society, or the Honors Program. Many Phi Theta Kappa members reached out to the program not only by becoming Peer Connectors, but also by encouraging eligible GED students to join and presenting the program's events and opportunities during the meetings. The guidelines for our plan proved to be most successful, and little did I know at the time how inspiring the program would become on our campus.

Initially, after the GED students started to meet with their Peer Connectors, I began to notice that many of them desired to be involved in other on-campus leadership programs as well, such as Phi Theta Kappa. By the end of the school year, many of them were eligible to join Phi Theta Kappa and the Honors Program. They quickly became a reflection of the people who invested time in them, not to mention how most strove for more leadership opportunities in their lives. I sincerely believe the Pathways to Persistence Scholars Program gave these GED students the confidence and resources they needed to achieve their personal and academic goals. The Peer Connectors in the program made the success of the GED students all the more possible and instilled in them a personal passion and desire for leadership and academic community.

Opening Doors for Leadership Growth

To help the Peer Connectors, I planned and led monthly meetings and set up weekly tutoring session times with the help of my advisor, Danielle Coronado, and Peer Connector representative, Camilo Romero. But it was not until Dr. Angela Long asked us to present the Pathways to Persistence Scholars Program to the American Association of Community Colleges and the U.S. Department of Education in Washington, DC, that I truly began to recognize the importance of this program and the impact it could make around the globe.

While in the nation's capital, we were able to express the great potential this program had for being implemented in other colleges across the country. After our last presentation, we toured the Arlington National Cemetery, where in my heart I thanked God for making dreams I thought impossible come to life. This glimpse of glory came through my own persistence, faith, and the direction of my mentors and family. I reached that peak, not on my own, but as a result of the people who trusted me to lead the student leadership component of this powerful program.

I was highly encouraged by the experiences I encountered through the Pathways to Persistence Scholars Program. I was also passionate about the program because of the effects it had on the other students involved as well. It gave us all a sense of hope and empowerment. Involvement in the program caused the students to look at their lives, abilities, and future in a different light. The future seemed brighter for everyone because success of the highest caliber seemed suddenly attainable. It developed within us a desire for success and provided a strong support group—a support group that felt like a family. It changed lives as the students discovered the strength they had within themselves to succeed in and outside of school. The mentors and leaders in the Pathways to Persistence Scholars Program nurtured the students involved to be the exception.

Give Others in Need the Opportunity to Lead

Most low-income students today lack opportunity, but the Pathways to Persistence Scholars Program presented opportunities for each of us that we thought would never be experienced. Specifically, at-risk populations need effective mentorship programs like this one to cultivate the success of so many individuals who do not have the resources to reach or maintain success on their own. Most of us have at least one person who motivates us or helps us at some point in our lives, and if we don't, we are more susceptible to failure. In my opinion, no one can reach success entirely on his or her own. I am a reflection of the people I encountered on my journey who touched my life and soul, and I know this is the case for many of the GED students in the Pathways to Persistence Scholars Program. They too needed student leaders and mentors to motivate and support them. Ultimately, the power of such a program is to allow students like myself to lead and work with other students to develop programs of retention. In doing so, connections are made at a deep level, which gives way to success and personal motivation.

Henry Wadsworth Longfellow (1836) once wrote, "Look not mournfully into the past, it comes not back again. Wisely improve the present, it is thine. Go forth to meet the shadowy future without fear and with a manly heart." My advice to each person reading this, whether administrator, faculty member, staff member, or student, is to celebrate the struggles that you have encountered so as to fully grasp the need for personal endurance that leads to success. Look on such with a keen eye in which to adjust and improve the present. Then, be a voice for those around you who are hurting and struggling to survive. Examine their hardships with the same focused eye and strive to impact their world by discovering and implementing ways to modify their excruciating circumstances. Give others in need the opportunity to be the exception and lead. For in doing so, each of us has the potential to change the educational outcomes of this nation.

References

Spotlight on Poverty and Opportunity. (2013). *Education and Poverty*. Retrieved, from http://www.spotlightonpoverty.org/education_and_poverty.aspx

Longfellow, H. W. (1836). *Hyperion: A romance*. Retrieved from http://www.online-literature.com/henry_longfellow/

PART FOUR

CONCLUSIONS AND RECOMMENDATIONS

WHERE DO WE GO
FROM HERE?

Angela Long

We were born to succeed, not to fail.

—Henry David Thoreau

On March 23, 2010, the Patient Protection and Affordable Care Act (PPACA), commonly called Obamacare, was signed into law. The PPACA enactment entails an annual expenditure roughly equal to one-sixth (16.6%) of the federal budget. Because of media attention to the PPACA, nearly every adult in the United States was aware of the basic framework of this legislation prior to its passage into law.

In stark contrast, few people know that roughly one-sixth (16.6%) of the American adult population has never obtained a high school diploma or a General Education Development (GED®) certificate (U.S. Census Quick Facts, 2012). Every day more than 8,300 teenagers become high school dropouts, adding to the already lengthy list of American adults who lack a high school diploma or a GED certificate[1] (U.S. Census, 2010). And even fewer people know that roughly 1 out of every 12 American adults have earned a GED credential in lieu of a traditional high school diploma.

When these numbers are conjoined and totaled, we find that nearly 60 million Americans have dropped out of high school; however, approximately 20 million of those individuals subsequently chose *not* to be labeled a high school dropout and voluntarily reinstituted their didactic formal training to obtain a GED certificate. Thus, when you walk into a large shopping mall, the odds are high that 1 out of every 5 adults you see dropped out of high school; however, of that total about 40% "dropped back in" to attain either a high school equivalency credential or a GED certificate.

There is ample anecdotal evidence that suggests the word *dropout* carries a pejorative connotation, not only within the domain of academia but also within the corporate world. And many people tend to stereotype high school dropouts as "quitters." Although it is true that GED completers dropped out of high school during one juncture in their lives, to group them under the heading of "quitters" is patently unfair. If a 16-year-old male dropped out of high school, then returned a few months later and persisted to earn his high school diploma (perhaps even becoming a member of the top 10% of his class), would we categorize that young man as a high school "dropout"? If not, then why do people tend to lump GED certificate holders together with high school dropouts? Inasmuch as government and education officials have jointly deemed the GED certificate to be the legal equivalent of a high school diploma, a student's acquisition of the equivalent educational document serves as prima facie evidence that this student should properly be viewed as a "completer," not as a "quitter."

The fact that GED certificate holders expend the time, energy, and money to enroll in a community college suggests that most of them likely believe a college education can help them obtain both better and higher-paying jobs. Given that fact, we are confronted with this perplexing oxymoron: Why would students who clearly recognize the importance of a college education suddenly walk away from their college experience within a few months after having been matriculated? Here is a befitting follow-up question: Over the course of the past 10 years, what percentage of community colleges have consistently tracked the attrition rates of their freshman GED students on a monthly basis?

The first question is too complex to be answered within the confines of a single chapter of this book. Nevertheless, there are five key methodologies that college personnel can employ that have the potential to dramatically enhance the persistence rates of their freshman GED enrollees. A brief overview of those five factors is given later this chapter.

Although the second question appears relatively easy to answer, it is not. National data dealing with this question do not exist. However, the odds are exceedingly high that the percentage of community colleges that kept accurate records on their GED dropouts over the course of the past 10 years lies somewhere between 0.1% and 1%!

There are a couple of statements in the introduction of this book that warrant reiteration in this final chapter:

1. "More than 40 percent of community colleges responding to a 2010 ACT survey have no one responsible for coordinating retention efforts; more than half have no goals for first-year student retention" (Jacobs, 2011).

2. "Data collection and data dissemination are still in the Dark Ages" (Schneider, 2011).

The 1996/2001 Beginning Postsecondary Study, conducted by the National Center for Education Statistics (NCES), was the first study that contained national data on attrition of GED certificate holders who enrolled as freshmen in the 1995–96 academic year in colleges and universities throughout the United States. Of more than 16,000,000 postsecondary students, the NCES 1996/2001 longitudinal study involved 12,083 individuals who were demographically representative of the American postsecondary universe. Of that total, 110 GED completers who enrolled in community colleges were chosen by NCES researchers to participate in the six-year longitudinal survey. But shortly after being matriculated, 14 of those students dropped out and never responded to the follow-up NPSAS:96 survey. During the 1995–96 academic year, another 23 GED students dropped out sometime during their first and second semesters. Thus, by the end of the 1995–96 academic year, only 73 GED survey respondents were still enrolled when the NPSAS:96 survey was taken.

Eight years after the onset of the aforesaid NCES study, the national *Crossing the Bridge* longitudinal study was launched. This particular study entailed a cohort of approximately 500,000 adults who tested for their GED certification in the 2003–04 academic year, and thereafter tracked them through the 2009–10 academic year. After matching data with the National Student Clearinghouse, the *Crossing the Bridge* researchers discovered that nearly half of the GED completers who subsequently enrolled in public two-year postsecondary institutions of higher learning walked away from the college experience either during or immediately after their first semester (Patterson, Zhang, Song, & Guison-Dowdy, 2010).

America's Forgotten Student Population

It was previously noted that 1 out of every 12 Americans is a GED completer. Moreover, research has shown that 1 out of every 8 entering students who enroll in postsecondary institutions of higher learning earned a GED certificate (Beginning Postsecondary Students Longitudinal Study; Zhang, Guison-Dowdy, Patterson, & Song, 2011). Given that second piece of information, it seems odd that the overwhelming bulk of community college administrators are unaware of the fact that, on average, about half of their freshman GED students drop out within five months after being matriculated. In terms of financial impact, a dropout rate of that magnitude means that a community college loses 6% of tuition revenue at the beginning of the second semester every academic year. But, in reality, the financial loss runs much deeper. Because of the first term attrition of half of all freshman GED students, the loss of tuition is compounded through the second, third, and fourth semesters. Here is the math: multiplying 325,000 GED students (half of all freshman GED enrollees) by an average credit load of 9 credit hours each totals 2,925,000 credits; multiplying $95 (the national average tuition fee per credit hour in 2010) by 2,925,000 yields a product of $277,875,000; multiplying $277,875,000 by 3 (i.e., the three subsequent semesters in which they did not enroll) yields a total dollar amount of $833,625,000. But this number is only part of the full impact inasmuch as a second cohort enrolls at the beginning of the second academic year. Hence, the loss of tuition dollars due to GED dropouts over a three-year period is more than $1,600,000,000! If prorated equally among America's 1,157 community colleges, each college would have enough extra money to hire 32 new full-time employees (based on inclusive payroll costs of $50,000 per employee).

An Internet search using key words such as *retention, persistence, attrition,* and *dropouts* is certain to produce a plethora of websites. Perhaps No Child Left Behind and Achieving the Dream are two of several initiatives on America's dropout crisis that have garnered the most media attention. Initiatives dealing with this topic focus on nearly every type of socioeconomic demographic imaginable: race, gender, age, financial status, ethnicity, and so forth. But the number of national studies that deal exclusively with both attrition and attainment rates of GED certificate holders who enroll in community colleges can be counted on the fingers of one hand. Because it is difficult, if not impossible, for community college policymakers to formulate an inexpensive retention metric for the GED demographic, where could they go to find in-depth, national data on this topic? A search on the Internet using the key words *GED, dropout, attrition,* and *persistence* produces little research.

As noted in the introduction, this book is to serve as a comprehensive resource for college administrators and government researchers who formulate policy. Certainly there is a sufficient amount of in-depth data contained in this book to enable policymakers to utilize it as a foundational stone upon which subsequent research can be built. The recommendations presented in this chapter are very effective in reducing first-semester dropouts among the GED demographic when administered by compassionate people.

Positive Versus Negative Attrition

The word *attrition* is commonly found in every study that has endeavored to identify reasons why students drop out of either high school or college.

This word denotes the conceptual meaning of a "wearing away" or "erosion" of some kind. Invariably, it goes without saying that high school and college administrators view student attrition as always being a negative thing. But in that regard, here is an intriguing question: Should it not be the goal of every high school principal to achieve a 100% attrition rate for each succeeding year's senior class? Indeed, why would any principal want to keep a single high school student from leaving school by means of graduation?

For community colleges to design an efficacious paradigm for enhancing student persistence, the term *attrition* must be redefined to mean one of these two things:

1. *Negative attrition*: Students who prematurely leave college prior to completing their educational objective
2. *Positive attrition*: Students who leave college after completing their educational objective

A community college's commencement ceremony is an apt example of positive attrition. Conversely, a newly enrolled freshman who drops out of college in the midst of his or her first semester is an example of negative attrition.

The paradigm that best serves to effectively bring about an overall increase in positive attrition must be based on methodologies that focus on positive actions. Doing nothing is a negative action. Inasmuch as the 2010 ACT survey revealed that more than half of all community colleges are lacking a metric that promotes first-year student retention, the fact that those colleges lose a significant number of their student bodies to negative attrition is understandable. Furthermore, when a community college adopts or emulates the marginally successful retention policies used by other colleges, then that, too, is a negative action. And, in the same vein of thought, if new policies are formulated to enhance positive student attrition but not implemented fully, then those new policies are just another way of doing nothing.

Five Factors for Improving Nontraditional Student Retention

The importance of the GED completer experiencing a positive first encounter with college personnel cannot be overstated. In essence, positive encounters produce positive results, whereas negative encounters bring forth ill will (at worst) or apprehensions (at best). Because many GED college students have been traumatized due to unpleasant experiences during their teenage years—unwarranted criticisms, mockery, taunting, bullying, and humiliations—they tend to be guarded, even somewhat distrusting, when meeting new people who are in a position of having control over their lives. For instance, first-time GED enrollees who lack adequate access to any needed student services (broadly ranging from academic counseling to financial advising) are left with the impression that the college environment is an uncaring and impersonal place. Indeed, even small acts of kindness and attention that are demonstrated by college personnel during the registration process, and that traditional high school graduates may barely notice, are almost always seen by GED students as outward signs of friendship and acceptance. Thus, if a GED certificate holder's first encounter with a college advisor or faculty member is friendly, the seedbed for future trust is planted at that very moment.

But as every college counselor and financial advisor has learned from experience, the hectic pace during registration week is not an ideal time for them to dedicate extra time or special attention to the needs of at-risk students. The crush of long lines of students waiting for assistance during the registration process causes college staff and students alike to become stressed out. But there is a significant difference between these two groups: All college staff earn money while enduring that hectic pace, whereas many GED students take unpaid time off from their jobs to wait patiently in line.

A young African American female I surveyed aptly summarized the feelings of many of her GED colleagues who became frustrated during the registration process. She had been standing in line for nearly an hour and a half, waiting to speak to a financial aid advisor, when another person in that department approached her and explained that she needed to go to the Student Advising Center and fill out forms before the financial aid advisor could see her. As instructed, she went to that office and again waited for an hour to talk with a counselor. But before she saw the counselor, an office worker explained that she needed to talk with a financial aid advisor first and was sent back to where she had started. She waited again, feeling "put off," "tossed around," and "angry." One of her cousins, who also had been waiting patiently, suddenly left his place in line and said to her, "College isn't worth it," as he walked out the door.

Simply put, counselors and advisors, not to mention faculty members, are limited in the amount of time they are physically able to devote to incoming students during the enrollment process. Therefore, the question is: When *is* a good time for a college to establish a good impression with the GED completer? By engaging those new students one or two weeks *before* they set foot on campus, the creation of a positive environment is almost a certainty. Which brings us to the discussion concerning an essential component needed for a community college's retention paradigm for at-risk students: the Friendship Factor.

In the following sections, I introduce theories and strategies that I have garnered through my own personal experiences working with GED student populations, through analysis of the many strategies contained within each chapter of this book, and through examples of various colleges across the country. The five factors I discuss have been formulated in an effort to lower rates of negative attrition, as well as provide potential recommendations that are worthy of consideration by state policyholders and college administrators when formulating new policies on this issue. Although these intervention strategies may not be the end-all solution to the attrition crisis, they have the potential to positively enhance a college's retention efforts.

1. The Friendship Factor

A friend is an ally, a supporter, a sympathetic listener, and a person for whom you feel fondness. An adversary is a person who opposes you, speaks unfavorably about you to others, and shows hostility toward you. And an indifferent person has neither positive nor negative feelings about you and sincerely does not care if you succeed or fail.

The fundamental objective of the Friendship Factor is to promote the imagery of a caring institution—a college wherein all employees, from its president on down through the ranks to the custodial staff, are collectively concerned about the academic prowess of their student body. And in order to optimize that image, there must be open channels of communication between students and the college's staff and faculty. Indeed, "friendship" is not built on the concept of being able to openly express one's feelings without concern of being unfairly criticized or mocked, but on the freedom to make mistakes without fear of ostracizing judgment. In essence, the key to opening the door to the friendship factor is for colleges to proactively strive to create a sharing, cooperative partnership—a team environment that celebrates development and growth not only for the students but also for the college itself and its personnel. The following strategies are useful in promoting an interactive environment:

- *Initiate positive first encounters.* Several weeks before college classes commence, it behooves college personnel to begin tracking the number of first-time enrollees on campus who earned a GED by compiling an accurate and complete listing of their names, residential addresses, e-mail addresses, and cell phone (or home telephone) numbers. Prior to the first week of classes, send out a written letter or e-mail message to all freshman GED students to personally welcome them to the campus, congratulate them on their decision to advance their education by enrolling in college, and invite them to participate in a special orientation session with college administrators and faculty. It is important that all GED enrollees be given printed information regarding any special college services or specialized programs that may be available for their use. Two or three days after the first contact, follow up with a personalized phone call or e-mail to confirm their participation at the special orientation session. At the session, allow students to sit down with faculty, advisors, and former GED students who have been successful in their studies, so that they can familiarize themselves with the college's campus and culture.

- *Register GED certificate holders together in a block of classes.* By registering students as a cohort, they will be guaranteed to have classes with students they already know or got acquainted with during the orientation session. Moreover, students taking two or more classes together can organize study teams in the form of learning communities. Mentors must engage GED students who attend the same classes to bond with one another and create lasting friendships throughout their college experience.

- *Assign each student a faculty/staff campus mentor.* Campus mentoring programs are crucial to providing the necessary support for nontraditional GED students. To establish such programs, colleges must recruit staff mentors who are willing to volunteer for 30 minutes per week over the course of a semester. Such mentors are selected from a list of employees on campus who match up to the career goals of the student. For example, a student interested in the nursing field would be assigned a faculty member from the nursing department. Campus mentors must sign a contract with their students and meet once weekly providing advising assistance, friendship, and guidance on college resources and activities. Typically, mentors are given a mentoring packet and invited to participate in a mentor luncheon with their newly assigned student at the beginning of each semester. Mentoring relationships can take place over one semester, one full year, or beyond. Over time, friendships are made and support networks are established to provide the critical support needed.

- *Create opportunities for students to connect with each other for support.* Most successful students find ways to engage with the campus environment. For many nontraditional students, the act of engaging on campus may prove challenging when outside demands require that their attention be placed elsewhere. Thus, colleges must create ways for students to connect with each other both in and outside of the classroom environment. Examples are support groups and student clubs created by the students themselves. Effective retention programs involve students in helping to recruit one another to be a part of such groups. Research has shown that when students discuss course content with others it guarantees that students will return to class. Colleges can assist GED cohorts in the creation of organized events that not only enable them to socially bond with each other but also serve to elicit a sense of responsibility toward each other. The hope is that after attending the first few events students will want to maintain these social networks.

2. The Financial Factor

Research has revealed that college students who lack funding to pay for their tuition and living expenses, regardless of whether they are nontraditional or traditional students, are at risk of dropping out of college. Similarly, there are many students who dream of obtaining a college education but dismiss that dream as pure fancy because they view themselves as indigent. Thus, the primary goal of the Financial Factor is to illuminate the pathway that enables underfunded GED completers to gain understanding and knowledge of financial aid opportunities at the very outset of their college experience, and to prepare them for the sundry costs of college. Generally speaking, GED enrollees have not been exposed to even a meager amount of financial literacy training. Most of them have little awareness of the several steps needed to apply for financial aid and charitable grants. Simply put, if GED students begin their college experience without having first been exposed to any type of financial literacy training, they tend to become discouraged quickly, causing them to drop out of college within a few months after being matriculated.

To address the financial needs of these students right away, implement the following intervention strategies, which have been proven efficacious by numerous community colleges for integrating the majority of nontraditional students into the college environment:

- *Provide assistance in the application process for financial aid.* GED enrollees view the application process for financial aid as both complex and cumbersome. Research has shown that the low take-up rate of the Pell Grant and Hope and Lifetime Learning tax credit programs is likely due to the complexity of the application process. For instance, the current Free Application for Federal Student Aid (FAFSA) comprises 102 questions that can take up to 13 hours to complete—longer and more detailed than a federal 1040 tax return. (We might easily suppose that the complexity of the FAFSA deterred more than 1.5 million *high school students* from applying for financial aid during the

2004 academic year, despite their eligibility for Pell Grant funding.)
One possible approach for ameliorating this perceived obstacle is to
have local tax return preparation businesses partner with community
college financial offices to jointly host group advising sessions during
the evening hours wherein students can receive guidance. (The benefit to the tax preparers is that some of those students will, later on,
become their clients due to familiarity.) Thus, when students meet
with a college financial advisor on their appointed day, the amount
of time they spend in that meeting is significantly reduced, as well as
their level of frustration.

- *Assign a financial aid mentor for each nontraditional student.* The fast-
paced environment of the financial aid office is not perceived as a
friendly environment by GED completers, who often easily become
frustrated or are emotionally insecure. Their initial objective of
pursuing all avenues of potential funding quickly shifts to a "get in,
get out fast" mind-set as they wait to speak with their financial advisor.
And because some of them have low self-esteem, they feel a sense of
embarrassment by having to "ask" for money, not to mention the
discomfort they might feel from revealing their low levels of income
(or types of income, such as child support and disability income) to
college officials, whom they perceive as authority figures. Perhaps it is
fair to say that a human trait shared by everyone is this: People prefer
to be in the presence of friends. For GED completers, the people
who worked with them in adult education centers are perceived
as friends—people who previously provided them with a relaxed,
familiar, and stable environment. Therefore, one feasible method
for putting the GED enrollees at ease is to establish a partnership
between the college's financial aid office and the area's adult education
center so that GED completers will receive a significant portion of
their financial counseling from the same people who helped them
obtain their secondary education credential.

- *Continue expanding Pell Grants for low-income students.* There are
both anecdotal evidence and limited research suggesting that Latino/a
students are more reluctant than other ethnic and racial populations
to become heavily indebted as a result of college loans. It might be
easily supposed that nontraditional students with children to feed
may have a similar mind-set in that regard, particularly if they already
have a long list of fixed debt obligations (e.g., mortgage payments,
auto loans). Such students rarely envision their college experience
happening on a full-time basis. Thus, they take one or two classes per
semester, believing the only possible way for them to obtain a college

education is to take five or six years of their lives to accomplish what a full-time student often finishes in two years. But there is ample research revealing that the longer the college experience is drawn out without attainment of a credential, the more likely the college experience will end by students permanently departing from their college experience without return. Interestingly, the 2013 NCES report entitled "The Condition of Education" shows that 20% of all community college students obtain either an associate's degree or a vocational certificate within three years after enrollment—a figure that aligns reasonably well with data showing that approximately one-third of all community college students receive Pell Grant funding.

- *Incorporate mandatory financial training workshops as part of a "first-year" seminar series.* Colleges can work with faculty and outside agencies to host a "first-year" seminar series in which students participate in a sequence of mandatory financial aid workshops highlighting the role of budgeting, cost analysis, and household finances. The workshops— evening seminars specifically designed for nontraditional GED students in their first semester of college—should include activities dealing with analyzing financial literacy profiles, gaining access to applications for scholarships and additional monies, and learning how to effectively balance a budget through interactive and hands-on lessons.

3. The Freedom-to-Fail Factor

Teddy Roosevelt once said, "Show me a man who has never made a mistake, and I'll show you a man who has never done anything." Indeed, who among America's most notable entrepreneurs never experienced a single failure while they were building their small businesses into corporate empires? Practitioners with years of classroom instruction similarly have observed students who failed tests miserably rebound from their failures to subsequently perform very well during their coursework examinations. But sometimes failure in the classroom is attributable more to one's mind-set regarding how to deal with a failing grade on a test than the innate intelligence or diligence in doing one's homework. Thus, the fundamental objective of the Freedom-to-Fail Factor is to communicate the notion that everyone is subject to failure, and that failure can be turned into either a negative or a positive experience—as well as a temporary or a permanent thing—depending on how one handles it. In other words, some perceive "failure" as something to run away from, and to blot out from one's memory, whereas others view it more positively and employ that experience as a guide to help discern the different pathways in life that lead either to disappointment or to success. Hence, it is critically important for GED completers (as well as all nontraditional at-risk students) to perceive failure as a learning tool rather than an ignoble thing. For many, failure may be a common theme experienced throughout life, and as such, it conjures up negative and demeaning self-perceptions. In that vein, the Freedom-to-Fail Factor is designed to encourage students who have been "knocked down," whether academically or emotionally, to stand again and turn that particular negative event into a positive learning experience. Following are a few methods whereby college personnel can help GED students develop a positive mind-set:

- *Promote the concept of risk-taking.* Taking risks of some type is an everyday occurrence for nearly everyone. People confronted with risk-taking decisions react in one of two ways: Some approach the decision by asking themselves, "What do I have to lose if I take this risk?" whereas others ask themselves, "What do I have to gain by taking this risk?" Within select programs on campus and in the classroom environment, faculty and staff must hold high standards of excellence for all their students, conveying the notion that true learning takes place in an environment of risk-taking where mistakes are bound to occur. Rather than experiencing a sense of loss and dejection from a risk-taking venture that failed, students must "seize the day," so to speak, and view that circumstance as an opportunity to gain another layer of wisdom (which almost always comes by means of experience). Simply put, positive thinking produces positive results, and vice versa. Thus, it is especially important for college faculty to constructively critique the academic performance of their GED students in a caring, positive manner; that is, pointing out deficiencies in need of improvement as helpful "coaches," not as uncaring "critics." In so doing, college educators will create an environment of risk-taking and provide the freedom for students to learn from their failures, not be crippled by them. Furthermore, within the classroom and college environment, faculty and staff should provide positive examples of leaders who have earned their GEDs and succeeded through great trials, such as Dr. Story Musgrave, U.S. astronaut; Dr. Bill Cosby of television fame; Senator Ben Nighthorse Campbell of Colorado; and Peter Jennings, former anchor of *ABC Nightly News.*
- *Establish academic advisement and early alert systems.* When a GED completer struggles academically in any given class, the issuance of a "midterm warning" by the instructor comes, as a general rule, too late for the GED student to salvage a high grade. More often than not, students tend to wait until the last minute to pull out of a class

in an attempt to avert a pending F on their accumulated GPA, or, worse yet, stop attending class altogether and simply walk away. Thus, that student drops out of college before the final examination is given, believing there is no hope to get a grade better than a D. As such, "early warning" systems are developed on the premise that intervention within the first month of enrollment is critical to coaching the student back on track when the student experiences failure. As previously noted, faculty can play a significant role in reducing the attrition rates of at-risk GED students by continually inculcating the notion that the best way to rebound from a troubling event is to treat it as another one of life's learning experiences that help to build wisdom. Some of the more notable telltale indicators that a GED student needs "early alert assistance" are irregular attendance or nonattendance, recurrent lack of preparedness for class participation, poor quality of written assignments, poor performance on quizzes and chapter tests, and expressions of mild anxiety or lack of confidence in completing college-level work. Faculty are asked to inform the appropriate administrator via e-mail or a phone call when they have concerns that a student is struggling and needs assistance. The action plan might include recommended hours spent studying in the learning resource center and working with peer tutors. If a student does not register for an upcoming term, it is recommended that college personnel send a letter informing the student that he or she is missed. Students, along with staff members, will be hired to assist with this program and will follow up with a telephone call to ask whether the student will be reenrolling the following semester.

- *Establish peer mentoring and peer tutoring programs.* The purpose of peer mentoring/tutoring programs is to connect newly enrolled GED students with other successful students (e.g., second-year GED student enrollees) who have completed at least one year of their college experience. Such partnerships allow the freshman GED students to learn from the prior year's cohort, who successfully persisted through their own frustrations and hardships during their first year as students. These peer mentors serve as a living example of the "If I did it, you can do it too!" archetype model. Needless to say, all student mentors and tutors selected from a previous year's cohort not only must have demonstrable academic prowess but also must be willing to undergo mandatory training sessions through the auspices of trained counselors. As part of their tutoring/mentoring duties, peer mentors will assist their matched peers by forming study groups, providing assistance with campus resources, and checking in via phone or in person at least once a week.

4. The Functional Factor

In her article entitled "The Challenge of Learning Communities as a Growing National Movement," Barbara Leigh Smith (2001), codirector of the National Learning Communities Project based at Evergreen State College, strongly recommended that whenever frustrated students on the brink of dropping out of college ask themselves the question, "Education for what?" the institution must have a retention rationale to assist those students in finding answers to their self-imposed query. Certainly a part of that rationale must include the notion of functionalism, that is, the practice of adapting method, form, and materials, primarily with regard to the purpose at hand. For example, the function of a student is to study. The Functional Factor is therefore squarely founded on the premise that students not only must have a stake in their own learning experience but also must serve as a functional component of the college's purpose. Thus, the goal of the Functional Factor is to engage students both on and off campus by providing opportunities for service, leadership, committee roles, and in-class teaching opportunities via means of a constructivist, hands-on approach. Hence, the college's role is to encourage its students to effectively and efficiently perform this function. Here are some ways in which this task can be accomplished:

- *Offer soft-skills courses that provide students with tips on note taking, test taking, communication, leadership, decision making, and stress management.* The goal of this particular act of intervention is to require students to take a first-year course or attend select seminars focused on soft skills learning as part of their first-year experience. Students who enter with documented deficiencies in mathematics and writing may enroll in a section that meets two days per week and provides a more intense focus on study skills, test taking, and time management. For these courses to be thought of as productive, students must be given the opportunity to interact and "teach" on the topic. A purely lecture-driven format is often nonengaging and irrelevant to the students' lives. Therefore, instructors need to teach according to a hands-on, constructivist-type model in order to help students learn and retain the necessary information. It is also recommended that any faculty teaching remedial classes provide their students with "comment cards" on a weekly basis. The purpose of these cards is to enable students not only to address presentations or discussions they found particularly intriguing but also to mention the things that they felt were confusing. Instructors can use the latter information to help those students who had trouble understanding the course materials during the next class.

- *Host an orientation week.* Hosting an orientation week for all first-time enrolled students just one week prior to the beginning of the first semester is an excellent way to engage students as functional members of the campus. Orientation week provides a variety of activities arranged for select days. During this week students review their program's purpose, the role of the student, services the college offers, and class schedules. Although a faculty meet-and-greet event may not strike either full- or part-time staff as particularly worthy of their time, their attendance creates a positive image of a caring college in the minds of the GED demographic, which pays big dividends later with respect to the college's persistence rates. Additional activities for the week can include a campus tour and an induction ceremony for all first-time enrolled students. It is recommended that family members be invited as guests of the enrollees, and that gifts of college promotional items be given to the incoming members of the class to welcome them to the orientation gathering.

- *Create opportunities for GED completers to serve the college.* To advocate for leadership opportunities, colleges must appoint GED students to task forces and committees that explore reasons why students drop out of college so that they can make recommendations to administrators with respect to how the college can improve retention. This specific objective will utilize the role of student government as well as members of the Student Life Department to recruit the GED population to serve on campus and be involved with the Student Life Department's activities. Colleges can use the power of student leadership and invite former GED graduates who have transitioned successfully through the postsecondary process to visit community programs, training facilities, Job Corps sites, and even prisons to share the value of moving forward in obtaining further credentials.

- *Tap into students' "multiple intelligences."* According to Howard Gardner, who developed the theory of multiple intelligences, there are eight types of intelligence (Gardner, 1983). These intelligences—musical, bodily/kinesthetic, spatial/visual, naturalist, linguistic/verbal, logical/mathematical, intrapersonal, and interpersonal—must all be taken into account before instructing and assigning tasks to adult GED learners. Allow the GED student to express himself or herself in a myriad of ways when completing assignments or presenting new information to others, rather than via means of the "paper-and-pencil" approach. Assess student learning gains, based on the multiple intelligences approach, by recognizing the individual potential of each student. Allow students to exercise their talents by participating in internship opportunities within the community, which may lead to potential future employment prospects.

5. The Fondness Factor

The goal of the Fondness Factor is, figuratively speaking, to make students "fall in love" with your college by celebrating the successes of individual students and by giving evidence of your appreciation and love for them. Create opportunities for students that encourage an atmosphere of excitement, engagement, and involvement in the campus experience. In essence, colleges must capture the hearts of their students by making it fun and exciting to be on campus. There is an old adage that says, "What is good for the goose is good for the gander." If we suppose that there is truth in this ancient saying, then when students love their campus and are engaged, it is assumed that the faculty on campus are having fun as well. When everyone is having fun, the campus environment takes on an exciting new life of its own. Creating an engaging environment involves not only community college faculty but also administration, staff, counseling personnel, and those within the financial aid and admissions offices.

- *Communicate to the nontraditional GED student that he or she is being inducted into an elite organization that truly cares about the welfare of its members—an organization always there to lift up any individual who stumbles and falls.* The college environment must be promoted in such a way that students feel it a privilege to be a part of the organization. By the very nature of the staff and faculty represented, colleges should treat their students as "royalty" and foundational to the success of the college. For this to take place, the administration, faculty, and staff must view themselves as capable leaders and their institution as an incredible place to be, work, and thrive.
- *Give GED or nontraditional students physical evidence that bears witness to their relationship with the college.* A caring relationship is often evidenced by some kind of outward sign or symbol, such as an engagement ring. Therefore, as members of an honored organization, students should be given promotional items as evidence of their positive relationship with the college. For example, articles such as T-shirts, key chains, hats, bumper stickers, padfolios, and book bags

bearing the college name display evidence that the student is officially a valued member of the school.

- *Hold outside and on-campus functions where students are welcome to bring their family and friends in order to incorporate them into the college atmosphere.* Incorporating family and friends in the celebration of one's college experience is critical. If students feel relaxed in a comforting atmosphere, that feeling will linger when they return to class, making them more comfortable on campus. It is important to include both faculty and staff during these events so as to foster the perception that faculty and staff care about their students, thus providing a positive framework for all future interactions. One way to include students' family and friends in the college experience is to hold cohort dinners to celebrate various events where students are honored and motivational speakers and other successful students relate their experiences and provide tips for college success. Through such interactions, students are able to experience a sense of pride as members of the campus environment while forging new friendships.

Final Recommendations

The ongoing problem of high attrition rates at two-year public institutions of higher learning can be likened to a coin laid flat on a glass coffee table. Adults will stand around the table and look down at that coin whereas small children are inclined to crawl under that table and gaze up at it. Both adults and children see the same coin, yet they see the two differing faces of that coin.

In the same fashion, the voices of the authors of this book include those of national researchers and seasoned educators as well as young people who are intimately familiar with the GED mind-set as a result of their personal experiences. The themes upon which each of the contributors focused pertained to characteristics of the GED demographic (and rightfully so). But I want to end this book by briefly looking at the other side of the "coin"—specifically, the forgotten aspect of high student attrition rates that researchers seldom address during their discussions on this topic.

In mid-May 2013, the NCES released a report entitled "The Condition of Education 2013." It makes the following statement of significant economic import: "In terms of student retention, among full-time, first-time students who enrolled in a postsecondary degree-granting institution in 2010 . . . 2-year public institutions had a retention rate of 59%." The reverse of this figure is 41%.[2] In other words, as a national average, 41% of all freshmen who enroll at community colleges leave after their first year.

It was mentioned earlier in this chapter that the annual loss of tuition revenue attributable to first-time GED students who drop out of community colleges exceeds $1,600,000,000. Thus, the question I now pose to college presidents and their top administrative staff is: If 41% of this year's freshman cohort drops out of college before next year, how many tuition dollars will your college lose? Given the fact that there are roughly eight times as many high school graduates as GED completers enrolled in community colleges, $1,600,000,000 multiplied by 8 amounts to a national loss of tuition dollars of about $13,000,000,000. Thus, if that 41% attrition could be pared by *just one-fourth* of that percentage, the resultant savings, if distributed equally to all 1,157 colleges, would be about $2,810,000 for each college on an annual basis.

Small private colleges depend on tuition fees to pay for a large portion of their operating expenses. On the other hand, tuition and fees account for 16% of the revenue collected by community colleges, with approximately 70% coming from state, local, and federal appropriations (College Board Advocacy & Policy Center, 2012). Thus, governmental sources currently pick up the bulk of the operational costs of community colleges. But that benevolence may be drastically reduced in the future. Indeed, an increasing number of state and local governments are beginning to experience budgetary woes due to employee pension funds. Therefore, colleges can benefit only by spending the time and effort to formulate new metrics and paradigms for student retention.

It is past time for our nation's policymakers to address the GED demographic that enters the community college portal with the hope of attaining an associate's degree or occupational certificate of achievement. If this book serves as an impetus to cause national policymakers to take notice of "America's Forgotten Student Population," it will be reward enough for the people who contributed to its writing. There are three specific proposals I would like to offer in that regard:

1. Establish a White House initiative that deals exclusively with the GED dropout crisis within colleges.
2. Replace the outdated appellation "General Education Development" (GED) with a new name more appropriate for 21st-century education that dispels all previous stigmas associated with the former title.
3. Formulate a national directive through the auspices of the U.S. Department of Education that requires all 1,157 community colleges to collect and report data on GED student attrition on a biennial basis to either the Institute of Education Sciences or NCES.

Some of education's most talented people are selected to work on White House initiatives that pertain to student persistence and academic excellence. Currently, there are initiatives dealing with the Latino/a demographic, the African American demographic, the Native American demographic, and the Asian American and Pacific Islander demographic. But where is the GED demographic? If the White House has an initiative addressing the Native American and Alaskan Eskimo demographics (approximately 4.1 million), surely a demographic comprising at least 20 million people is worthy of the White House's attention.

The purpose of national data is to allow local entities to see how they compare to national and regional medians. Briefly stated, the U.S. Department of Education is the most practical source to gather that data from local entities. It is my hope that someone in that department will heed the recommendations in this chapter.

In many respects, this book is the seminal resource for people who need national data on GED persistence rates in community colleges. More often than not, the difference between students who achieve academic success and those who drop out of college is not distinguishable as much by intellect as it is by attitude. Henry David Thoreau, one of America's greatest philosophers, was correct when he stated, "We were born to succeed, not to fail." The concept of Thoreau's statement rests at the very core of this book and, as such, has the potential to awaken in the lives of millions the hope for a restored future.

Notes

1. The analysis of 8,300 is a comparison of enrollment status data of the U.S. population 3 years of age and older from 2000 to 2010, Table 1—Enrollment Status.

2. The 41% attrition rate presented in the NCES 2013 report on all full-time, first-time enrolled students at two-year public colleges excludes students who transfer.

References

College Board Advocacy & Policy Center. (2012). *Trends in college pricing 2012.* Retrieved from http://advocacy.collegeboard.org/sites/default/files/college-pricing -2012-full-report_0.pdf

Gardner, H. (1983). *Frames of mind: The theory of multiple intelligences.* New York, NY: Basic Books.

Jacobs, J. (2011, December 16). Study: Community college dropouts prove costly. *U.S. News & World Report.* Retrieved from http://www.usnews.com/education/

best-colleges/articles/2011/12/16/study-community-college-dropouts-prove
-costly

National Center for Education Statistics (NCES). (2013). *The condition of education 2013*. [Data file]. Retrieved from http://nces.ed.gov/programs/coe/indicator_ctb .asp

Patterson, M. B., Zhang, J., Song, W., & Guison-Dowdy, A. (2010). *Crossing the bridge: GED credentials and postsecondary outcomes (Year 1 report)*. Washington, DC: American Council on Education. Available at www.gedtestingservice.com

Schneider, M. (2011, October). The hidden costs of community colleges. *American Institutes for Research*. Retrieved from http://www.air.org/files/AIR_Hidden _Costs_of_Community_Colleges_Oct2011.pdf

Smith, B. L. (2001, Fall). The challenge of learning communities as a growing national movement. *Peer Review*. Retrieved from http://www.aacu.org/peerreview/ pr-fa01/pr-fa01feature1.cfm

U.S. Census. (2010). *Enrollment status* [Data file]. Table 1. Retrieved from http:// www.census.gov/hhes/school/data/

U.S. Census Quick Facts. (2012). *Educational attainment* [Data file]. Retrieved from https://www.census.gov/hhes/socdemo/education/data/cps/historical/index.html

Zhang, J., Guison-Dowdy, A., Patterson, M. B., & Song, W. (2011). *Crossing the bridge: GED credentials and postsecondary educational outcomes: Year two report*. Washington, DC: American Council on Education.

Top 100 Postsecondary Institutions Transitioning GED® Passers to Own PSE Programs: 2004

Name of Institution	State	Total GED® Passers Enrolled in PSE	Total GED® Passers Enrolled at the Same Institution	Transition Rate (%)
University of Alaska Anchorage	AK	254	236	92.9
Northwest Shoals Community College–Muscle Shoals	AL	188	163	86.7
Northeast Alabama Community College	AL	106	84	79.2
Jefferson Davis Community College	AL	83	67	80.7
Bevill State Community College	AL	194	149	76.8
North Arkansas College	AR	121	94	77.7
Mid-South Community College	AR	66	54	81.8
Black River Technical College	AR	63	48	76.2
Yavapai College	AZ	182	156	85.7
Central Arizona College	AZ	251	207	82.5
Imperial Valley College	CA	111	95	85.6
College of the Desert	CA	66	56	84.8
Allan Hancock College	CA	89	65	73.0
Trinidad State Junior College	CO	170	140	82.4
Otero Junior College	CO	139	110	79.1
Northeastern Junior College	CO	62	49	79.0

(*Continues*)

Name of Institution	State	Total GED® Passers Enrolled in PSE	Total GED® Passers Enrolled at the Same Institution	Transition Rate (%)
Colorado Mountain College	CO	177	135	76.3
Pensacola Junior College	FL	169	128	75.7
Indian River State College	FL	248	209	84.3
Florida State College at Jacksonville	FL	858	668	77.9
Daytona State College	FL	491	375	76.4
South Georgia Technical College	GA	250	191	76.4
Flint River Technical College	GA	81	60	74.1
Kirkwood Community College	IA	221	177	80.1
Indian Hills Community College	IA	156	120	76.9
Hawkeye Community College	IA	118	100	84.7
College of Southern Idaho	ID	257	224	87.2
Southwestern Illinois College	IL	398	372	93.5
Sauk Valley Community College	IL	163	141	86.5
Parkland College	IL	82	69	84.1
McHenry County College	IL	174	136	78.2
Kishwaukee College	IL	89	66	74.2
Kaskaskia College	IL	113	95	84.1
Illinois Valley Community College	IL	113	95	84.1
College of Lake County	IL	759	652	85.9
College of DuPage	IL	547	444	81.2
Carl Sandburg College	IL	54	41	75.9
Black Hawk College	IL	122	95	77.9
Ivy Tech Community College–Central Indiana	IN	68	52	76.5

Name of Institution	State	Total GED® Passers Enrolled in PSE	Total GED® Passers Enrolled at the Same Institution	Transition Rate (%)
Garden City Community College	KS	60	49	81.7
Cowley County Community College	KS	70	62	88.6
Butler Community College	KS	54	40	74.1
Southeast Kentucky Community and Technical College	KY	174	157	90.2
Madisonville Community College	KY	107	80	74.8
Hazard Community and Technical College	KY	127	99	78.0
Greenfield Community College	MA	81	62	76.5
Cape Cod Community College	MA	97	80	82.5
Berkshire Community College	MA	120	87	72.5
Delta College	MI	51	41	80.4
Southwest Mississippi Community College	MS	66	53	80.3
Northeast Mississippi Community College	MS	103	76	73.8
Mississippi Gulf Coast Community College	MS	436	347	79.6
Meridian Community College	MS	194	144	74.2
Itawamba Community College	MS	259	194	74.9
Hinds Community College	MS	171	141	82.5
East Mississippi Community College	MS	64	48	75.0

(*Continues*)

Name of Institution	State	Total GED® Passers Enrolled in PSE	Total GED® Passers Enrolled at the Same Institution	Transition Rate (%)
Wilkes Community College	NC	85	65	76.5
Tri-County Community College	NC	55	46	83.6
Rowan-Cabarrus Community College	NC	215	171	79.5
Rockingham Community College	NC	81	65	80.2
Pitt Community College	NC	120	87	72.5
Piedmont Community College	NC	94	76	80.9
Guilford Technical Community College	NC	208	156	75.0
Gaston College	NC	169	128	75.7
Davidson County Community College	NC	83	63	75.9
Cape Fear Community College	NC	113	87	77.0
Bladen Community College	NC	50	42	84.0
Alamance Community College	NC	200	159	79.5
Northeast Community College	NE	80	59	73.8
Metropolitan Community College Area	NE	227	168	74.0
Mercer County Community College	NJ	90	68	75.6
San Juan College	NM	179	170	95.0
Eastern New Mexico University–Roswell Campus	NM	402	297	73.9
Clovis Community College	NM	122	93	76.2
Shawnee State University	OH	64	48	75.0
Lorain County Community College	OH	188	142	75.5

Name of Institution	State	Total GED® Passers Enrolled in PSE	Total GED® Passers Enrolled at the Same Institution	Transition Rate (%)
Cuyahoga Community College District	OH	217	171	78.8
Portland Community College	OR	777	673	86.6
Linn-Benton Community College	OR	255	204	80.0
Lane Community College	OR	155	113	72.9
Chemeketa Community College	OR	333	245	73.6
Chattanooga State Community College	TN	292	220	75.3
Texas State Technical College Harlingen	TX	181	140	77.3
Southwest Texas Junior College	TX	126	104	82.5
Odessa College	TX	101	79	78.2
Navarro College	TX	59	49	83.1
Del Mar College	TX	350	268	76.6
Amarillo College	TX	118	91	77.1
New River Community College	VA	65	53	81.5
Wenatchee Valley College	WA	162	129	79.6
Walla Walla Community College	WA	436	365	83.7
Shoreline Community College	WA	107	82	76.6
Seattle Community College– South Campus	WA	113	92	81.4
Seattle Community College– North Campus	WA	142	103	72.5
Lower Columbia College	WA	174	150	86.2
Columbia Basin College	WA	367	300	81.7

(*Continues*)

Name of Institution	State	Total GED® Passers Enrolled in PSE	Total GED® Passers Enrolled at the Same Institution	Transition Rate (%)
Bellingham Technical College	WA	146	133	91.1
Southwest Wisconsin Technical College	WI	96	84	87.5
Fox Valley Technical College	WI	383	330	86.2
Casper College	WY	101	83	82.2

ABOUT THE CONTRIBUTORS

Helton "Hep" M. Aldridge, EdD, served as the project coordinator for a statewide college completion initiative entitled "Finish Up Florida!" through the Florida Department of Education. In this capacity, Dr. Aldridge traveled across the state of Florida to counsel college institutions on the process of helping former dropouts reenroll in college and developed a system for colleges to follow (more than 79,000 students had been identified as dropouts). Because of his efforts, in one year, more than 11,500 students who were in this cohort completed their degree and another 12,600 are currently reenrolled. As an innovator in his field, Dr. Aldridge has presented nationally and internationally on the topics of student success and student persistence. Prior to his work with the Florida Department of Education, he retired as dean emeritus from Brevard Community College in Cocoa, Florida. He holds a BS in social science from the University of Central Florida, an MA in higher education administration from Norwich University, and an EdD in policy and foundations from the University of Florida. He is a U.S. Air Force veteran and has received multiple statewide honors including the Florida Association of Community Colleges (FACC) State Exemplary Practice Award and the FACC Student Affairs Administrator of the Year award in 2007.

Margaret Becker Patterson, PhD, has more than 10 years of research administration experience at the state and national levels, ran a statewide research and data analysis consulting business for seven years, and has presented extensively around the country. Dr. Patterson served as director of research at GED Testing Service® from 2008 to 2011. During the three years that she oversaw the research activities at GED Testing Service, the research team authored more than 20 research reports; compiled numerous statistical reports on national General Education Development (GED®) test taking; and initiated two major groundbreaking studies, one quantitative and the other qualitative. *Crossing the Bridge* established a national college-going rate for GED credential holders for the first time, using records from more than 1 million test takers. *Perceptions and Pathways* was a six-state study that Dr. Patterson led in 2011 and was deemed the largest of its kind in the United States. Dr. Patterson is a passionate leader and cutting-edge thinker who has devoted numerous hours to address the needs of adult learners in this nation.

She holds a PhD in education research from the University of Kansas, as well as an MA and a BA from Pennsylvania State University. Currently, she actively consults as a senior researcher through Research Allies for Lifelong Learning (R-Ally™) in the Washington, DC metro area.

Pamela Blumenthal, MA, is the director of alternative programs at Portland Community College (PCC) in Portland, Oregon. She is a leader and innovator in education who is passionate about creating equity and opportunity for underserved student populations. Pam began her work at PCC leading the Gateway to College program, which started in Portland and has been replicated across the United States. She now leads a group of dedicated staff in five programs designed to support at-risk students in achieving college success and completion. Pam is actively involved in local and national initiatives focused on education reform. Prior to her work at PCC, she was a counselor and administrator in K–12 education settings. Pam earned a BA from the University of Oregon and an MA in counseling psychology from Lewis and Clark College.

Catlin Cade, AA, is a 2012 Santa Fe College graduate currently attending the University of Florida to pursue a bachelor's degree in elementary education in addition to a master's in special education. She is a first-generation college student and active representative of low-income learners. While at Santa Fe College, Catlin served as the Peer Connector Coordinator for the Pathways to Persistence Scholar's Program. In this position, Catlin demonstrated her passion for education by assisting the Peer Connectors and GED students in the program. Additionally, Catlin was chosen to present information on the student leadership components of the program to the American Association of Community Colleges (AACC) and U.S. Department of Education in Washington, DC. Catlin has been recognized for her great volunteerism in the community as a tutor and mentor, and in 2012 she received the Santa Fe College Hall of Fame award, given to the top one-tenth of 1% of all students at the college.

Steve Dobo, MEd, is the CEO and president of Zero Dropouts, an organization with national scope addressing the high school dropout crisis. Zero Dropouts utilizes innovative technology, social media, and new marketing techniques to creatively reduce dropout numbers in cities, states, and school districts across the country. In developing creative "Drop In" campaigns first piloted in Colorado, Steve has pioneered new approaches to reaching out and intercepting students who have dropped out in order to help them return to school. Steve founded Colorado Youth for a Change (CYC), a nonprofit organization dedicated to solving Colorado's high school dropout crisis, and has operated it for the past eight years. Other work that Steve has done in his 30-year career involves work with homeless teens and families, parents in poverty, and youth at risk of education failure in varied settings of municipal government, school districts, and nonprofit organizations across the country. Steve earned a BA in physics from the University of North Carolina at Chapel Hill and an MEd in counseling from Colorado State University.

Mark A. Heinrich, PhD, is chancellor of the Alabama Community College System. Dr. Heinrich holds a PhD in counseling from the University of Alabama and earned BS and MA degrees in psychology from Tennessee Tech University. During the time he was completing his graduate degree at the University of Alabama, Mark served on Coach Paul Bear Bryant's staff as an academic counselor and tennis coach. Before returning to Tuscaloosa in January 2008 as president of Shelton State, he worked for Carson-Newman College in Jefferson City, Tennessee, as a faculty member and administrator. In addition to positions in academia, he worked as a private practitioner in psychology and serves on numerous community and academic boards. Throughout his career, Mark has been very involved with all aspects of accreditation, strategic planning, program and curriculum development, budget planning and development, enrollment management, and many other administrative responsibilities typically associated with higher education. As an educational leader, Dr. Heinrich places a high value on participatory governance and team-based leadership, a foundational philosophy he sees as essential in his role as an effective and successful leader of the Alabama Community College System. He believes strong college-community relationships are paramount to the health of the system's institutions and critical to the economies of their local communities.

Angela Long, EdD, serves as an independent researcher, educator, and consultant on nontraditional student retention issues in higher education. Dr. Long helped found the Pathways to Persistence Scholars Program at Santa Fe College in Gainesville, Florida. The Pathways Scholars program was a first-of-its-kind program aimed at increasing the persistence and retention rates of students with GEDs at the postsecondary level with emphasis on scholarship and student leadership. Angela is the author of the Five Factors theory for increasing nontraditional student retention and speaks nationally on this topic. She has participated in three White House summit meetings on educational excellence for Hispanics and has shared her findings before participants at the Achieving the Dream national conference; the Florida Association of Community Colleges; the U.S. Department of Education; the White House Summit Meeting on Educational Excellence for Hispanics in Miami, Florida; the Consortium for Student Retention and Data Exchange;

the American Association of Community Colleges; and the Florida Council of Student Affairs, to name a few. Dr. Long holds a doctorate of education in community college leadership from Oregon State University, and both a master's of education in school counseling and consultation and a bachelor of arts in elementary education from Northwest Christian University. She has experience teaching as a practitioner in the K–college setting and was the first to publish a national document, entitled "Community College Attrition of GED Certificate Holders and Regular High School Graduates: A Comparative Study Using National BPS Data," that sought to compare national attrition rates of all students at the community college level.

Christopher M. Mullin, PhD, serves as the assistant vice chancellor for policy and research at the State University System of Florida, board of governors, where he provides leadership and direction with regard to academic and student affairs policies and programs, strategic planning, research, analysis, and special projects in support of the board of governors' constitutional responsibilities. Prior to joining the board, Dr. Mullin served as the program director for policy analysis of the American Association of Community Colleges (AACC) in Washington, DC. In this capacity his chief responsibility was to provide analysis and supporting data with an emphasis on federal student financial assistance, accountability, institutional performance, college costs, and related institutional policies. Additionally, he responded to immediate needs for the analysis of federal legislative, regulatory, and related policies while also playing a central role in shaping AACC's longterm federal policy agenda. He has taught at the early childhood, elementary, middle, and high school levels as well as at three universities. His work has been reported in the *Wall Street Journal, The Chronicle of Higher Education, Inside Higher Ed,* and *Education Week,* as well as on *NBC Nightly News.* Dr. Mullin interacts regularly with members of national media including but not limited to the *CBS Evening News,* the *TODAY Show,* the *New York Times,* the *Wall Street Journal, Bloomberg News,* and the *Huffington Post.* His completed research has been published in more than 30 policy documents, 14 articles in peer-reviewed journals, and 5 book chapters. He has given more than 70 presentations at the national, state, and local level. Dr. Mullin serves the postsecondary community in many ways, including on the editorial advisory boards of *Journal of Education Finance, Community College Review,* and *Community College Journal of Research and Practice,* and as the coordinating editor of the peer-reviewed *AIR Professional Files.* Dr. Mullin earned a BA from the University of Florida in 1999; an MEd from Teachers College, Columbia University in 2005; and a PhD in higher education administration from the University of Florida in 2008.

Story Musgrave, MD, a former U.S. astronaut, was born in 1935 on a dairy farm in Stockbridge, MA. Experiencing hardship growing up, he dropped out of high school and enlisted with the U.S. Marines where he served as an aircraft electrician and engine mechanic in North Korea. After earning his GED, Dr. Musgrave went on to obtain a BS degree in mathematics and statistics from Syracuse University (1958), an MA in business administration in operations analysis and computer programming from the University of California at Los Angeles (1959), a BA in chemistry from Marietta College (1960), an MD from Columbia University (1964), an MS in physiology and biophysics from the University of Kentucky (1966), and an MA in literature from the University of Houston (1987). He has been awarded an additional 20 honorary doctorates from various universities across the United States. For over 30 years, Dr. Musgrave served as a NASA astronaut and flew on six spaceflights. He performed the first shuttle spacewalk on *Challenger's* first flight, was a pilot on an astronomy mission, conducted two classified DOD missions, was the lead spacewalker on the Hubble Telescope repair mission, and operated an electronic chip manufacturing satellite on *Columbia*. Furthermore, he was the communicator in mission control for 25 missions. Over his 58 year flight career, he accumulated approximately 18,000 hours in over 160 aircraft. He has received many special honors including the National Defense Service Medal and an Outstanding Unit Citation as a member of the United States Marine Corps Squadron VMA-212 (1954); Reese Air Force Base Commander's Trophy (1969); NASA Exceptional Service Medals (1974 & 1986); Flying Physicians Association Airman of the Year Award (1974 & 1983); NASA Space Flight Medals (1983, 1985, 1989, 1991, 1993, 1996); and, NASA Distinguished Service Medal (1992). In 2003, Dr. Musgrave was honored to be included in the NASA Hall of Fame. Today he is a producer/director of multimedia, a landscape architect, an innovator with Applied Minds Inc., and a professor of design at Art Center College of Design in Pasadena, CA.

Frederick Parks Jr., BS, is a 2010 graduate of Santa Fe College with a background in biotechnology and agriculture. He graduated from the University of Florida in the fall of 2012 with a bachelor's degree in pre-professional biology. Fred has been involved in various medical research projects concerning nosocomial infections, winning an undergraduate microbiology poster fair and establishing a sepsis-related protocol. Currently, he is working at Shands Hospital at the University of Florida's Academic Health Center while applying to medical school in order to continue pursuing his goal of becoming a medical researcher with an intense focus on oncology. During the 2009–10 academic school year, Fred served as the director for external affairs in Student Government and diligently represented the voice of the student body before local and statewide governmental bodies. Fred has represented the student voice by helping to speak on behalf of GED students at community colleges and is a cofounder of the Pathways to Persistence Scholars Program in Gainesville, Florida. During his time as a student representative of the Pathways project, Fred helped to assist in the development of the program by working with administration to establish the various pillars of its layout, including mentoring, tutoring, and working as a teaching assistant.

Leah Rapoza, MA, is a first-generation college student who earned her GED from Portland Community College in 2003. Not long after, Leah enrolled in Portland Community College's nationally recognized Gateway to College program and graduated in 2008. Since then, she has excelled in her academic studies and has earned a bachelor's of social science (2010) and a master's of education (2011), both from Portland State University. As Leah was growing up, her family struggled with poverty and moved often. Due to outside family circumstances, Leah was removed from her formal education at the age of 6 and homeschooled until the age of 10. Despite these trials, Leah's love of learning remained steadfast throughout her adolescent years. To date, Leah has become a leader in education and displays her passion daily for children, especially those struggling in poverty. Leah works as a teacher in the Portland area school district and is an ice-skating coach in her spare time. Currently, Leah is pursuing a second master's degree, in special education, and is expected to graduate in March 2014.

Jackson Sasser, PhD, president of Santa Fe College since 2002, is an innovator of the community college system as it relates to national economic security in the higher education system in America. Under his leadership, Santa Fe College was named one of the top 10 colleges in the country by the Aspen Institute. Dr. Sasser, one of the first in the United States to define community colleges as essential to national economic security, believes that the role of community colleges should be to educate workers necessary for American business and industry to succeed globally. He is a leader of Innovation Gainesville, a community-wide initiative that quickly converts university research into products that succeed in world markets and provides well-paying jobs. Dr. Sasser previously served as president of Lee College in Baytown, Texas, and interim president and vice president at Calhoun Community College in Decatur, Alabama. He was 2008–9 chair of the Board of Directors of the League for Innovation in the Community College, 2007–8 chair of the Florida Community College Council of Presidents, 2006–7 president of the Florida Association of Colleges and Universities, and 2003–4 chair of the AACC Presidents Academy.

Wei Song, PhD, is director of data and analytics at Achieving the Dream, a national reform network dedicated to community college student success and completion. Dr. Song oversees the Achieving the Dream and Completion by Design databases and identifies strategic use of these data. Wei was director of research projects at the Council of Independent Colleges (CIC), overseeing CIC's three assessment consortia and institutional benchmarking services. She previously worked for the American Council on Education's GED Testing Service for five years, first as a research associate and then as assistant director for data management and research. Wei holds a PhD in public administration and an MA in international development from American University.

Also available from Stylus

Working With Students in Community Colleges
Contemporary Strategies for Bridging Theory, Research, and Practice
Edited by Lisa S. Kelsay and Eboni M. Zamani-Gallaher
Foreword by Susan Salvador
Afterword by Stephanie R. Bulger

"This is a valuable resource that will help readers to understand community colleges and the needs and characteristics of their students as well as help to gauge how agile and responsive these colleges are to demands and changes.

These chapters provide a timely and valuable resource for the array of professionals working to adapt and evolve their practices in an exciting and challenging time for community colleges. The comprehensive treatment of institutional operations and student progress makes this reading an important resource for practitioners, administrators, and faculty. In addition, this book provides insightful strategies and recommendations for strengthening student services and identifying internal and external barriers for change and partnerships.

If you embrace our responsibility to serve the community college student sector effectively, you will turn the pages of this book with the realization that it is a necessary instrument for the community college professional's toolbox."

—*Susan Salvador*,
Vice President of Student Services, Monroe Community College

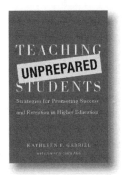

Teaching Unprepared Students
Strategies for Promoting Success and Retention in Higher Education
Kathleen F. Gabriel
Foreword by Sandra M. Flake

"An invaluable tool for college and university faculty whether or not they teach unprepared students. It is a primer for all of us who believe in the value of a rigorous education that fosters development of knowledge and skills for a lifetime. It does so by recognizing that students learn better in an environment where they understand the expectations, where they learn through application and practice, and where multiple pathways to knowledge and skills result in lifelong learning and education. That is also why this book provides useful ideas for those of us engaged in working with a full spectrum of students, from the unprepared and often unengaged to the well-prepared and dedicated learners. Gabriel recognizes there are multiple paths to successful learning, and faculty members can guide students to finding the pathways that help them to be successful."

—*Sandra M. Flake*,
Provost and Vice President for Academic Affairs, California State University, Chico

22883 Quicksilver Drive
Sterling, VA 20166-2102   Subscribe to our e-mail alerts: www.Styluspub.com